GOD CALLS
MEN TO
MOVE BEYOND...

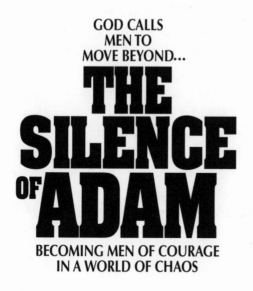

THE SILENCE OF ADAM

BECOMING MEN OF COURAGE
IN A WORLD OF CHAOS

Other books by Larry Crabb

Basic Principles of Biblical Counseling
Effective Biblical Counseling
Encouragement: The Key to Caring (with Dr. Dan Allender)
The Marriage Builder
How to Become One with Your Mate
Men and Women: Enjoying the Difference
Inside Out
Understanding People
Finding God
God of My Father (with Lawrence Crabb, Sr.)
The Adventures of Captain Al Scabbard (with Lawrence Crabb, Sr.)

GOD CALLS
MEN TO
MOVE BEYOND...

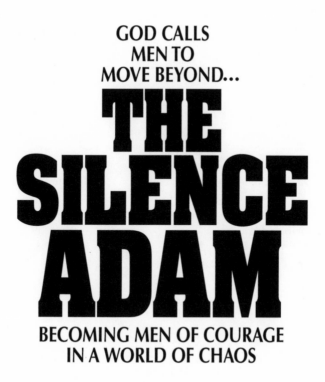

THE SILENCE OF ADAM

BECOMING MEN OF COURAGE
IN A WORLD OF CHAOS

Dr. LARRY CRABB

WITH DON HUDSON & AL ANDREWS

ZondervanPublishingHouse
Grand Rapids, Michigan

A Division of HarperCollins*Publishers*

The Silence of Adam

Copyright © 1995 by Lawrence J. Crabb, Jr., Ph.D., P. A., dba, Institute of Biblical Counseling

Requests for information should be addressed to:
  Zondervan Publishing House
  Grand Rapids, Michigan 49530

Library of Congress Cataloging-in-Publication Data

Crabb, Lawrence J.
    The silence of Adam : becoming men of courage in a world of chaos / Larry Crabb
  with Don Hudson and Al Andrews.
        p. cm.
    ISBN 0-310-48530-4
    1. Men (Christian theology)   2. Men—Psychology.   3. Role expectation.
  4. Men—Religious life.   I. Hudson, Don, 1959–   .   II. Andrews, Al, 1954–   .
  III. Title.
  BT701.2.C83 1955
  248.8'42—dc20   94-47627
                                                                          CIP

    International trade paper edition 0-310-48539-8

Edited by John Sloan
Interior design by Joe Vriend

Printed in the United States of America

95 96 97 98 99 00 / ❖ DH / 10 9 8 7 6 5 4 3 2 1

This edition printed on acid-free paper and meets the American National Standards Institute Z39.48 standard.

To Our Sons
Kep and Ken
Michael
Hunter
May we father you well

Table of Contents

Acknowledgments

Thanks to:

John Sloan, who edited this book, and the entire Zondervan team. Always a pleasure to work with. Integrity defines them.

Sealy Yates and Tom Thompson, brothers in ministry who disguise themselves as literary agents.

Sandy Pierce, a woman who wears many hats and wears each one well: sister in Christ, close friend, personal assistant, colleague, encourager; and who, by the way, typed the manuscript, along with Cindy Skelton. Cindy, thanks for your hard work, time, and support.

Rachael, Suzanne, and Nita, our wives, who gracefully endure our struggle to become godly men and who make the struggle worthwhile. Women of beauty deserve men who move. We want to move toward you all the days of our lives.

Our fathers—Larry, Sr., Donald Eugene, and Andy—men who walk the path ahead of us and encourage us to follow.

Adam Remained Silent When He Should Have Spoken

Where was Adam when the serpent tempted Eve? The Bible says that after Eve was deceived by Satan, she took some of the forbidden fruit ". . . and ate it. She also gave some to her husband, WHO WAS WITH HER (emphasis added), and he ate it" (Genesis 3:6).

Was Adam there the whole time? Was he standing right next to his wife while the serpent tricked her with his cunning? Was he there, listening to every word?

If he was—and there is good reason to think so—then a big question must be asked: *WHY DIDN'T HE SAY ANYTHING?*

Before God created Eve, he had already commanded Adam to never eat from a certain tree. Adam was expected to pass on the prohibition to his wife when she appeared on the scene. We assume he did so.

But when the serpent struck up a conversation with Eve designed to muddle her thinking about God's goodness, Adam said nothing. Yet he was listening to every word! He heard Eve misquote the command of God that he, Adam, had carefully communicated to her. He was watching when she began looking at the forbidden tree. He saw her take a step toward the tree and reach out to pluck some of its fruit. And he didn't do a thing or say one word to stop her. Adam remained silent! Why?

Remember, Eve was deceived by the snake, but Adam wasn't (1 Timothy 2:14). He knew what was going on. Perhaps he should have said, "Now, wait just one minute here! Honey, this snake is up to no good. I can see right through his devilish cunning. He's deceiving you into thinking you have more to gain from disobeying God than by remaining faithful to him. That's a lie!

"Let me tell you exactly what God said to me before he made you. And look around us. This is Paradise. God made it and gave it all to us. We have no reason to doubt his goodness." And then, turning away from Eve: "Snake, this conversation is over. TAKE OFF!"

But Adam said nothing. He stood there, heard and watched the whole thing, and didn't say a word. He failed his woman. He failed, in his first spiritual struggle, to represent God. He failed as a man!

The silence of Adam is the beginning of every man's failure, from the rebellion of Cain to the impatience of Moses, from the weakness of Peter down to my failure yesterday to love my wife well. And it is a picture—a disturbing but revealing one—of the nature of our failure. Since Adam every man has had a natural inclination to remain silent when he should speak. A man is most comfortable in situations in which he knows exactly what to do. When things get confusing and scary, his insides tighten and he backs away. When life frustrates him with its maddening unpredictability, he feels the anger rise within him. And then, filled with terror and rage, he forgets God's truth and looks out for himself. From then on, everything goes wrong. Committed only to himself, he scrambles to make his own life work. The result is what we see every day: sexual passions out of control, uninvolved husbands and fathers, angry men who love to be in the driver's seat. And it all began when Adam refused to speak.

Men are uniquely called to remember what God has said and to speak accordingly, to move into dangerous uncertainty with a confidence and wisdom that comes from listening to God. Instead, like Adam, we forget God and remain silent.

And Satan keeps winning too many victories: in our society, in our churches, and in the lives of our wives, children, and friends. It is time for men to recover their voices, to listen to God—and to speak.

INTRODUCTION

This book is written by three growing but struggling men—men who openly confess that our struggles seem to deepen as our lives continue. Our lives are simply not together the way the Christian culture seems to think they should be. Christian men, especially those in leadership, are expected to feel consistently encouraged, to be passionate about their vision, and to have very few problems. Mature men aren't supposed to struggle with crazy thoughts, sinful urges, or despairing feelings. But we think they do.

Our view of spiritual manhood has more to do with continuing to function in spite of difficulties than with successfully overcoming them. We believe that God's Spirit is less interested in telling us how to get our lives together, and more concerned with stirring—in the middle of our ongoing difficulties—our passion for Christ. Rather than solving our problems, he more often uses them to unsettle us, to make us less sure of how life works, to provoke us to ask the hard questions we're terrified to ask, to surface the stubborn doubts and ugly demands that keep us distant from Christ.

We don't believe the Bible provides a plan for making life work as we think it should. We think it offers a reason to keep on going even when life doesn't work that way. If we could find formulas that actually worked—formulas for getting over anger or producing godly kids or feeling closer to our wives—we'd follow them. But we don't think they exist. In our thinking, real men admit their fear of confusion but don't run from it into an easy confidence or step-by-step plan.

We're more drawn to the mystery of life than to its predictability. Not because we especially like feeling confused and out of control. It's hard to feel that way. Sometimes we hate it. But we don't think we have a choice, not if we're honest with ourselves as we face life.

Some parts of life, of course, are orderly and manageable. Cars don't run without gas; flossed teeth develop fewer problems; families don't get along as well without an involved husband and father. Things that are doable should be done. Where life can be managed, it should be managed well.

But the most important parts of life, those parts that make up what Christianity is all about, seem to us more mysterious than manageable, more chaotic than orderly. What do you do when you find out your daughter was sexually abused by a baby-sitter? How do you handle nagging jealousy toward a friend who makes more money than you do? What can you do with an immoral fantasy life that just won't quit? How do you get close to God when everything inside feels dead? How does the Spirit of God bring us to the Father's home, where the party is going on?

There simply aren't any formulas to follow in handling the things that matter most. And we think God designed it that way, not to frustrate or discourage but to call something out of us that he has already put in us, something that is released only when we abandon ourselves to him in the midst of mystery. Spiritual manhood involves the courage to keep on moving—in the middle of overwhelming confusion—toward relationships. It has little to do with figuring out exactly what works and then doing it.

We write this book as three men living out unfinished stories. We wrestle with questions no one answers. We fail in ways we thought we'd be done with by now. We battle ugly desires within us, including the urge to quit when life wears us down. We struggle to live in community with each other.

But still we're hopeful. Maybe our lives are moving toward a kind of maturity that will open our mouths and leave Satan speechless. We entertain that hope because, even though we're confused, sometimes discouraged, and occasionally desperate, we're still moving toward our wives, our kids, our friends, and our God.

We don't always move well, and at times we stop. But never as a permanent adjustment. And this is our core message: MANHOOD MEANS MOVING—not always success, not even victory, but moving, the kind of movement that only a passionate, consuming, Spirit-directed fascination with Christ can produce. And that is true victory.

Permit us to introduce ourselves to you: three men, each with a story to tell—stories of sadness, joy, failure, success, boredom, passion, vengeance, and love. Join us in thinking through what it means to be a man, to live as God intended men to live.

THE STORY BEGINS

LARRY CRABB

The kid in the front row with the rascally grin—that one on the far left—is me at age four. It is a strange feeling to look at myself nearly fifty years later and wonder what lay behind that attention-grabbing smile. My mind drifts from that picture and wanders off in several directions.

I remember when I was about thirty. I had just led a Bible study in Phil and Evelyn's living room. During the social time that followed, I grabbed a piece of Evelyn's cake and made the rounds. I can see myself joking, teasing, entertaining—engaging each of the folks I had just taught, with what my memory tells me was a noisy grin, not unlike the one in the picture. After everyone left but my wife and I, Evelyn approached me with a knowing, somewhat troubled look.

"I think I know why you act like a clown sometimes," she said.

I immediately felt caught, more than a little unnerved. But I managed to remain casual. "Okay, why?"

"Because it relieves the pressure of being the man you are."

Another memory. I was maybe twelve. On vacation with my parents and brother, I was spending the night in a log-cabin motel in the mountains of upper New York, just outside the sleepy village of Schroon Lake. My bed was the top bunk. A window opened onto the moonlit lake bordered by a thousand pine trees.

I remember lying on my bunk, staring out the window, utterly caught up in the majesty of the scene. An irresistible sense that I was part of something big, something beautiful, crept into my awareness. In all my life, it was perhaps the closest thing to a call from God I ever heard. I knew that I fit, I knew that I was part of a larger story, and I felt stirred. I had something to give that would make a difference.

I was thrilled, excited; I felt lifted up into a dimension I had never before seen. But I was also frightened, terrified with a fear that wanted to paralyze me.

Another memory comes to mind as I write. As a child growing up in Plymouth Meeting, a tiny suburb of Philadelphia, my bedroom was at the end of a long hallway. One night I was lying in bed, reading my Bible. I was perhaps thirteen. I heard Dad's footsteps coming toward my room. I quickly hid my Bible beneath the sheets and grabbed a comic book.

Dad would have been delighted to see me reading the Bible. Why did I deny him that joy? Why did I prefer to be seen with a comic book?

Ask Mother what I was like as a youngster, and—as she has done many times—she will immediately reply, with a look of fond exasperation, "He was a rascal!"

During my growing-up years, all the way through high school and college, I worked hard to be silly. No one who knew me then ever guessed that I felt called by God and that I read my Bible. The fact that I write serious books rather than cartoons has surprised most of my teenage friends.

Have I been trying for years, from kindergarten on, to hide my substance behind nonsense? Did I joke with our Bible study friends to keep them from taking me too seriously? Did the notion that I had something to say to this world terrify me? Was I a rascal in order to run away from a primitively sensed calling to be a man, to deny the dreams that were forming within me?

Maybe I'm still a rascal, still grinning as I sit in the front row of my community. I wonder if the prospect of moving into my world as the person I know I am still terrifies me, perhaps enrages me, and leaves me feeling isolated, disconnected, lonely. These thoughts enter my mind as I stare at the grinning four-year-old that was—and perhaps still is—me.

As I keep looking at the picture, an entirely different line of thinking comes to mind. I have no recollection of it, but I cannot imagine the Sunday school teacher was especially pleased with my rascally smile. If I close my eyes and visualize her presumed disapproving look, I can feel a strange pleasure, a definite feeling of satisfaction. I've never felt I was a part of my peer group. I've never easily bowed beneath standards. Perhaps I like it that way. A little rebellion tastes good.

Maybe there is a good kind of rebellion, a spunkiness, a courage to live authentically, even at the cost of not fitting in. Maybe it is the courage to dream. Whatever it is, I like it.

A little honest reflection makes me think I'm an iconoclast, a nonconformist, a radical with short hair and a navy blazer. A seminary employed me as a professor for seven years—and then asked me to leave. My presence did not sit well with some of their constituency. Looking back, I can see a hundred things I said and did that would understandably trouble them. Many of those things were immature, and some were sinful; a few I would do again.

Releasing who I am feels like dangerous business. I just may be a rebellious rascal, with a mischievous grin on my face, more often than I realize. But neither rebellion nor rascalness defines me. Something else is more central to my being. I am a masculine reflection of the character of God.

I was designed to move into and through my world with laughter and hope. I am called to concern myself less with conformity than with integrity, less with fitting in and more with the visions of a dreamer. The lightness of hope's laughter and the courage to stand alone as dreams are pursued are marks of a man.

Clowning is cheapened laughter. Clowns smirk. Men laugh. Rebellion is corrupted integrity. Rebels destroy. Men give life. I want to be neither clown nor rebel, but I do not want to avoid these two errors so rigorously that I lose the good qualities they disguise. I do not want to be a predictable conformist, caught up in something that requires less of me than I am called to give. I don't want a fantasy life that I can enjoy without ever getting off the couch. I want dreams that get me moving in the face of impossible odds.

I want to hope when life is intolerable, and I want to disrupt what makes it intolerable. Maybe the attention-grabbing grin of the rebellious rascal will one day mature into the laughter of a romantic and the courage of a dreamer.

DON HUDSON

God made man because he loves stories.

Elie Wiesel, *The Gates of the Forest*

I have felt like an impostor most of my life. So I wear a nice suit, assume a successful posture, put a smile on my face, look like I have it together. I am the picture of success. But don't let the picture in this book fool you. There is another picture I never show anyone. If you saw me as I see myself, you would see a different person. You would see a man who feels insecure and incompetent, a man who loses hours of sleep at night because he is worried about being successful. You would see a man who believes that he has nothing to offer, so he must pretend that he has something—any-thing—to offer. You would see a man who wonders if there is anything underneath the nice suit.

The boy in a suit: an excellent portrait of my life as a man. I pretend I have it together on the outside, while I am falling apart on the inside. I was six years old when this photograph was taken, and it was not long after my parents' separation. As I entered first grade, I wanted to identify with my dad so much that I changed my first name to my father's. Incredible: a six-year-old changing his name. But that is what I did. No longer would I be Michael Hudson; I would be Donald Hudson.

I distinctly recall the stark emptiness of our home, how I missed my father and longed for him to be with us. I dreamed that he would return someday. I also feared for my mother's welfare. For the first two weeks of first grade, I would secretly slip from class and run back home out of concern for my mother. While the rest of my friends were at school, laboring over their ABC's, I was fretting over how we were going to make it in life. A six-year-old boy became a little man. I was caught between the need to be a man for my mother and the loneliness of being a little boy without a father.

I was not a man, nor did I feel like a man, but that did not matter. What mattered most was that, as a young boy, my world crumbled beneath my feet, and I was confronted with horrifying chaos. My circumstances forced me to invent some way of coping with my terror, confusion, and sadness. But how could I cope if there was nothing to fall back on? How could I be a man, when in reality I was a little boy? I was convinced that being a man was impossible, like trying to draw life-giving water from an empty well. Thus, the impostor began his journey.

This was how I lived as a young boy, and this was the way I chose to grow into manhood. Most men seem to face marriage, children, vocation, and finances with great ease; I faced them with paralyzing fear. For instance, marriage was an agonizing decision for me, one I flirted with for years. I would date someone for a few months or a few years, and then—as the prospect of marriage loomed closer and closer—suddenly, miraculously, I would conjure up doubts "from God." And they were convincing. They included questions like whether, as my wife, she could live in a trailer, eking out a living on a pastor's salary, or wondering (after a few months of dating) what happened to the "chemistry" we once enjoyed?

My pattern of dating was so predictable it was frightening. The closer someone came toward my heart, the more fiercely the doubts rushed in, and the more quickly I ran. I was running at a dead heat; from what, I did not know—but I was running. I always excused myself by glibly explaining to people that this was just my personality. "Hey, I'm a free and easy guy." But I could not escape the suspicion that I was running from the very things I wanted most. Even though I was terrified, I knew that I desperately longed to love and be loved. I passionately desired to share my life with someone special, someone who would walk the journey with me. I loved children, but I never believed I could be a father.

To compensate for my fear and my feelings of incompetence, I followed the pattern I learned as a child: I discovered a way to *feel* like a man. By the time I reached twenty-eight, I had realized many of my vocational dreams. I was competent and successful in my ministry. I threw myself into my work with a fearsome vengeance. I lived to compete and win, and I would overtly dare people to tell me that I could not accomplish any task. I would prove them wrong every time. Same picture, just a little older—nice suit, nice-guy smile, successful posture.

But something was terribly wrong. I was successful but empty. The more I excelled in work and education, the more I felt that I excelled in things that did not matter. I crawled through the maze that society sets before its men, and I came to a dead end. Much worse, I was a dead end. Secretly, I lived with this motto: "I do not have what it takes to be a man in my world." All my energy was spent convincing everyone that I was worthy because I was competent. My well was empty, and I was attempting to fill it with things outside of me, things not really important. Living and loving cost a million dollars, and only a few pennies jingled in my pocket.

If I were to stop here, though, my story would be just one more tragedy. In this book, we make much of stories. One of the major reasons for doing so is our conviction that we are a generation of men without stories. We are a generation of men who do not know who we are, why we are here, or where we are going. All of us are on this journey called manhood, but few of us, if we are honest, feel at ease with the path we tread. Because I did not have the privilege of growing up with my father, I didn't believe I had any story to fall back on, any story to carry on. I felt that no one was for me, so I had to be for myself.

The absence of story in my life has driven me back to the remarkable story of my Father, the one who was always there. And I have discovered that I do have a story to tell. Out of my loss has arisen a rich and varied story. Now I can see a little more clearly that my story is all about the redemptive, disabling touch of a Father; it is a story that has given courage to a terrified man, confidence to an insecure man, and hope to a discouraged man.

If we sat down for coffee and you looked at me today, you would see a strange picture indeed. From time to time you would see the boy who defrauds you with a suit and a smile. You would still observe a boy who fears and falters. But more times than not you would see a man—not a boy—who has changed dramatically. You would talk to a man who loves his wife and is utterly taken by his son. You would see a man who has a few close friendships, and a man who no longer alienates his father, whom he loves.

I used to think that being a real man was springing out of bed every morning with a perfect story—no fears, no tragedies, no insecurities, no self-doubts. But now I believe that to be a man in this world is to be one who has courage to overcome his fear, faith to answer his doubts, and love to get him beyond his loss. Hope, for me, lies in my potential to redemptively touch people for generations to come rather than merely brushing by them like a driven phantom.

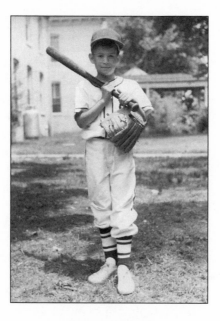

AL ANDREWS

The framed black-and-white photograph of the Little Leaguer rests on the top of a dresser in our bedroom amid other family memorabilia. The familiar striped uniform, capped head, and bat-over-the-shoulder pose will, I imagine, be viewed by my grandchildren one day in the distant future.

I wonder how they'll look at me. Will they look at the picture with the same disinterested gaze that I often have when perusing old family albums? Will they laugh at the "old-fashioned" uniform and at the ears protruding from an oversized cap? They might laugh, but I hope they do something different. I want them to know something more. My desire is that they understand that this photograph is but a single frame from a long-running movie and cannot be understood out of the context of the entire film. I want them to wonder about that boy. What was he like? What were his strengths, his failures, his dreams?

How I will pass that sense of history on, I'm not exactly sure. But I am certain that before I pass something on, I have to know it myself. In a sense, I must become keenly interested in that photograph before I ask someone else to ponder it. I want to understand the scenes of my past in the larger context and then to see how they fit within a greater picture, a movie that was running long before I was born and will continue on forever.

That's why I want to be a part of this book. Because I want to think about my own story in a way that makes a difference to those with whom I am in relationship—my wife, my family, my friends, and my colleagues. I want to think of my story not in some self-absorbed way but in a way that leads to change.

The picture on the dresser is reflective of what I mean. It is a photograph of me, eight years old, dressed and ready for the game. That's what you can see. What you cannot see is a kid who didn't excel at team sports. And what you also cannot see—what even I could not see for years—are the deep commitments in that Little Leaguer's heart to a particular way of life. Let me explain.

I will never forget my first time at the plate. After tryouts and months of anticipation, I was where I had dreamed I would someday be. I was at bat. The pitcher that day was one of the larger eight-year-olds: at that time, an intimidating figure. The first pitch, a swing and a miss—strike one. The second pitch, arguably not over the plate but called good—strike two. The third pitch, way to the left—ball one. The fourth pitch, a swing and a miss— strike three! I don't remember my failure as a terribly unusual or difficult experience; strikeouts were pretty common among the Angels.

As the weeks went on and my strikeouts continued, however, I do recall a strange feeling beginning to come over me. Many of the other guys on the team were starting to get hits. And with the hits came cheers and yells and jubilant runs around the bases. While they were enjoying the game, I had not yet connected a ball with a bat. Gradually my thrill and enthusiasm for the game had given over to embarrassment and drudgery. It began to look as if the season might be a long one, at least for me.

And then I noticed something. Some guys were able to get on base without making a hit. They were the batters who had more balls pitched to them than strikes and were then allowed to walk to first base. Now and then they were even able to enjoy the thrill of the cheers as they pounded the bases on their way toward home, the result of a good batter who followed them in the batting order.

Striking out became more and more humiliating, so I made a decision, though I do not recall it being a conscious one. Given the fact that Little League pitchers were not known for pinpoint accuracy, I realized there was a good chance that a number of the baseballs hurled in my direction would miss the strike zone. If I didn't swing, at least I'd have a chance to get on base, and I could put a stop to that awful feeling that came with striking out. For the rest of the season, I never swung the bat again. Pitch after pitch after pitch, the bat rested on my shoulder. And though I struck out more than I had hoped, I got on base now and then. On occasion I made it home.

That story is a sadly fitting metaphor for how I chose to live much of my life. For many years, even as an adult, I had a strong commitment not to swing the bat, because swinging was too painful. When a man swings and misses, he knows failure and humiliation. Incompetence is exposed and shame is the by-product. Even if he swings and hits, he feels the pressure of expectations. After all, if you hit once, you should be able to hit again. It is easier to rest the bat on your shoulder and wait for the occasional walk, dependent on the failure of the pitcher and the next batter's success. The thrill of rearing back, following through, and hitting a ball over the fence is, for many men, unthinkable.

It was the picture of my life: a man standing still, afraid to move, refusing to move, wanting to move, holding back because of a greater and prior commitment to safety, whether in vocation, in relationships, or in the responsibilities of daily life. And any observable successes that were gained were attributed to others and, internally, viewed with suspicion.

As I write these words, I have a sense of both sorrow and joy. Sorrow for the harm that my lack of movement has inflicted upon others. Sorrow for living so much of my life apart from God's intended design for me as a man. Regret for years spent in chosen and seemingly necessary impotence.

If that were the end of the story, I'd have no reason to write. But a pen is in my hand and it is moving. I have come to know the sensation of a swing and a hit, and in the process, what I feared has indeed occurred. Failure has been more than evident, and the pressure that comes with doing well has only increased. But passion, which was killed by my lack of movement, has come alive, and with it has come a desire for more.

PART 1

Something Serious Is Wrong

The Dream Is Lost

Men are easily threatened. And whenever a man is threatened, when he becomes uncomfortable in places within himself that he does not understand, he naturally retreats *into an arena of comfort or competence, or he* dominates *someone or something in order to feel powerful. Men refuse to feel the paralyzing and humbling horror of uncertainty, a horror that could drive them to trust, a horror that could release in them the power to deeply give themselves in relationship. As a result, most men feel close to no one, especially not to God, and no one feels close to them.*

Something good in men is stopped and needs to get moving. When good movement stops, bad movement (retreat or domination) reliably develops.

Chapter 1

A Vision for Men

Married less than two years. And things were terrible. He felt lost, confused, angry. All he knew for sure was that he wanted to talk to his dad. More than anything, he wanted his dad to understand, to be there with him, to look on him kindly, with involvement and respect, to neither lecture nor shrink back.

His father had always been his hero, the model for everything good. Successfully married for thirty-four years to his faithful mother, a woman who never complained, who always stayed at home. He could remember hearing her express interest in working at the nearby children's hospital— she really liked kids—but his dad always brushed her aside with a smile and a gently reproving reminder that he would provide for his family.

At church, too, his dad was a wonderful example. An elder, he served the elements at the monthly Lord's Supper, fought to keep the midweek prayer and Bible study when the new associate pastor suggested home groups instead, never drank (everyone knew it), faithfully tithed, held family devotions most every night, kept three children always under control. "Your family is such a good testimony" was a phrase he often heard addressed to his dad, who always smiled and gave God the glory.

Why did the twenty-minute drive to his father's home seem so long? Why the terrible tightness in his chest?

"Dad," he began, "I've got to talk to you. Things in my marriage are really horrible. I don't know what to do."

The smile. That same smile that kept his mother at home for thirty-four years. The same one that others thought humble. He realized then, for the first time, how much he hated it.

His dad spoke: two book titles, followed by advice to read Ephesians 5, then the suggestion that he commit everything to the Lord.

"But, Dad!" he nearly exploded. "I've read the books, I've studied Ephesians 5, and I've prayed as best I know how. *I want something more from you!*"

His father sat still. The smile faded, replaced by a look that could kill, a look he had seen before but never directed at him. Silence. A terrifying moment of tension, then his father stood up and, without a word, left the room.

"That was the first time," he later admitted, "I realized my father was a weak man."

I wonder what it would look like to see a man who was utterly abandoned to God.

On the wall next to the desk in my office, the words of D. L. Moody hang written, framed, and positioned so that I see them every day:

> The world has yet to see what God can do with and for and through and in and by the man who is fully and wholly consecrated to Him. I will try my utmost to be that man.

I love to read biographies, the stories of men like Oswald Chambers, C. S. Lewis, John Knox, Jonathan Edwards, Augustine, Paul, and Jeremiah. As I read about their lives, I get the impression that our modern ideas about masculine maturity are a far cry from what godly men of earlier generations understood and practiced.

We talk a lot today about things like vulnerability and the courage to feel our pain. *They* seemed more interested in worship and witnessing. *We* speak of honest communication and living up to our potential. *They* fell to their knees in brokenness and got up to serve.

I wonder if the virtues we try to develop came naturally to those men from years ago whose toughest battles were fought against whatever kept them from knowing Christ.

We get together in small groups to share our feelings and to discuss principles for relating more intimately or building self-esteem. *They* took long walks with older men who spoke easily about God and broke into prayer without warning.

During his "dark night of the soul" (which lasted several years), Oswald Chambers was out shooting rabbits one day with John Cameron, an old friend from Scotland, accompanied by two dogs. The purpose of the hike was to hunt, but when they came upon a grassy bank, Cameron suggested they stop for a while and pray.

"We knelt down and he led in prayer," Chambers wrote of the occasion. "Then I began to pray, but the young collie dog, who had been perfectly quiet during the old man's prayer, imagined I was meant for nothing but to play with him, and he started careening around, pawing me all over, licking my face, and yelping with delight. Cameron rose from his knees, sternly took the dog by the neck and said 'Hoot, hoot, I will sit on the dog while you pray.' And he did."[1]

Religious men of today too often have found a convenient God, an immediately useful God promoted by leaders who are filled more by the thrill of adoring crowds than by their opportunity for quiet communion with God. The most enduring sin in Israel's history was committed by King Jeroboam (see 1 Kings 12, especially verses 26–33), who made it easy for people to worship, by reducing God to a local, visible deity; and he did it solely to advance his own ambitions. It worked. He won a big following and reigned in Israel for twenty-two years.

Big crowds can produce good things. But they scare me. God's deepest, most enduring work is more often done in isolation, in one-on-one dialogue, or in small-group discussion. Sometimes his best work begins in big crowds, but what happens there can easily be mistaken for something finished, when it is no more than something begun.

Big crowds help modern men feel like men. Whether we're rooting for our football team or cheering the name of Jesus, we handle our emptiness by filling ourselves with whatever excitement we can find. Huge rallies pump us up with what feels like authentic manhood.

Men from earlier generations slugged it out in intensely personal battles that lasted for years, battles that lessened only when they abandoned themselves more fully to Christ, not merely when they felt a new passion sweep through them at a big rally or when they discovered some new insight about themselves in therapy. The joy of finding Christ was released through brokenness over sin, brokenness that led to worshipful abandonment to God. Knowing Christ intimately developed through a deep work of God's Spirit that took place sometimes in big crowds but more often during long seasons of agonizing prayer in solitude.

It can be argued that men today tend to be more relationally sensitive than our stern forefathers. Perhaps we are more aware of "connecting" with our wives, children, and friends. Maybe we are learning that real men are both tender and strong, in ways that older men never clearly understood.

The modern counseling movement can claim a good share of the credit for that good effect.

But whatever gains we have made in modern society have been largely stripped of their value, because most of us have lost the depth of connection with Christ that only comes through unexplained suffering, excruciating brokenness, and deep repentance.

This book is a call to return to old paths, not to give up the good lessons that modern Christian thinking has taught us but to go back to a much stronger focus on finding ourselves by losing ourselves in Christ. I want to see us push aside our efforts to solve our problems, heal our pain, and recover our self-esteem! I want to clear the stage for Christ to fill the spotlight; I want to fix our attention so completely on his beauty and power that every other thought is scented with his fragrance.

Worshiping him, praying to him, eagerly looking for him throughout all the Scriptures, humbling ourselves before him in brokenness over our pride and our lukewarm devotion, waiting upon him to fill us with his Spirit, serving him with single-minded purpose and a passion that consumes all others: these are the old paths to which we must return.

As you read this book, do not lose sight of one simple truth: *The only way to be manly is first to be godly*. In our day, men are looking for their manhood more than they are seeking God. Too many men make the mistake of studying masculinity and trying to practice what they learn, without paying enough attention to their relationship with God. Do we really love Christ, or is our passion more contrived and wavering than genuine and steady? Are we growing in a holiness that draws others (particularly our families) to Christ, or do we exhibit a fervency—and practice a conformity—that merely impresses others with our zeal?

Ron was part of a weekly, early morning men's group at his church. They talked about battles with lust, tensions at home, worries at work. They prayed and sang together, they embraced one another and sometimes wept, they held each other accountable. Ron always left these meetings pumped up and ready, as a man, to take on his world. He couldn't have been more surprised when his wife asked him one day to stop attending the group. She didn't like its effect on him. She felt he came away more excited than tender, more resolved to do the right thing than to involve himself with his family and friends.

Our best efforts to become manly will never produce authentic manhood until an abiding sense of worship grows in our hearts. And if we think that finding Christ is something we can do at a weekend seminar, then our worship will be shallow. Finding Christ is a long, pride-crushing battle that leads through despair to the unmanageable joy of Spirit-fulness and then back again through darker despair to an even brighter joy. Men who avoid that battle will experience only surface repentance. Their real commitment will be to things that don't really matter. They will never develop a passion capable of touching the center of anyone else with life-giving love.

Ron did quit the group. He began meeting for breakfast with an older gentleman in his church whom he had noticed for years but had never known. Ron had heard him pray many times in church. His prayers were different. They seemed like intimate conversations with a much-loved friend. For nearly four months, Ron met with this man, sometimes every week. He asked him to talk about his life, his marriage, his relationship to God. The man always brought his Bible and often opened it with the excitement of a grandfather pulling out pictures of his first grandchild. When the older gentleman could no longer meet as regularly, Ron's wife was disappointed.

Men who learn to be fascinated more with Christ than with themselves will become the authentic men of our day. Men of this generation must learn to count the cost of following Christ (the cost is easily calculated: everything we have); we must feel the emptiness of our souls until no cost seems too high if it brings us into contact with him; we must resist the influence of a "Christian" culture that values self-discovery and self-fulfillment above abandoning ourselves to God. To put it simply, we must be more concerned with knowing Christ than with finding ourselves.

If all this actually happens, then thirty years from now more children might find, in the older generation, more examples of godly, manly men. They might be drawn to seek God with all their hearts and souls, because of the powerful consistency and nonthreatened love that they see in us.

I have a dream. Only time will tell if it is truly from God. I think it is.

My dream is really quite simple. As I look thirty years into the future, I see a few groups scattered here and there, across the Christian landscape, where *godly character and spiritual wisdom are more honored than degrees and skill, and more valued than achievement or expertise.*

OF ADAM

I see a community of struggling people, plagued with all the ills that come from living in a world we were never designed to endure, battling against inclinations and urges we were never intended to feel. I see people whose marriages are awful, whose children have shattered their hope for a happy family, whose emotions are out of control, who spend horribly long nights terrified by childhood memories of unspeakable abuse, who feel so hurt by rejection that it seems their hearts are being torn right out of their chests, who hate themselves because of the sexually perverted urges that rage within them, who come close to giving up all hope under the weight of never-ending loneliness.

In my dream, I see these people doing something that very few are doing today in real life. I see them walking past the office that has a shingle advertising a professional whose training guarantees technical competence but not godly character. I see them returning books to the shelf of the Christian bookstore: the books with jackets that falsely promise now what only heaven will later provide. I see them picking up a flyer promoting the seminar everyone is talking about, looking at it, then putting it down.

I see these people stumbling into the living room of the lonely widow, making their way to the coffee shop to spend a couple hours with the tired widower, knocking on the door of the study where someone waits who is clothed with humility and eager for heaven, someone who is unself-consciously faithful as he warmly points to Christ.

I envision a generation in which mentors are not in such short supply, in which pastors and elders are once again held in high esteem because they pastor and elder, in which Christian leaders are no longer asked to manage ministries the way executives build corporations, but rather are revered as men of godly influence. If I look hard into my dream, I can see an army of wise men and women distributed among God's people, armed only with gentle discernment and penetrating wisdom, character qualities that have been forged in the fires of suffering. These are the ones who have paid a price few are willing to pay. And they have paid it continually for years, without relief. These men are FATHERS, these women are MOTHERS, godly people whose quiet presence is felt and valued.

A young couple wrote me in desperation. "We've been married six years and it's just not working. Do you know a good Christian therapist in our area?"

Why would this couple write to me, a trained, licensed, professional psychologist, rather than ask an elder in their church to meet with them? Were they drawn by my title? By my character? Why do most people with problems think immediately of getting "professional help"? Why don't they turn to wise Christian men and women? Most of us would no more consult an elder in our church for help with panic attacks or sexual struggles than we would ask a pastor to perform a root canal. Why?

Our culture has bought the lie that personal problems are no different in nature than physical problems. In both kinds of problems, we think something is wrong that can only be fixed by an expert whose understanding exceeds the wisdom provided in the Bible. We have entirely lost sight of the fact that every nonphysical problem is, at core, a moral problem,[2] with its roots in a person's relationship with God.

We have therefore produced a generation of therapists, an army of counselors trained to do battle with problems they poorly understand because they have spent more time in classrooms becoming experts than in God's presence becoming elders. We have lost interest in developing mentors, wise men and women who know how to get to the real core of things and who have the power to bring supernatural resources to bear on what's wrong.

If my dream comes true, our entire culture will shift. Like an earthquake that dramatically changes the landscape, so my dream, if realized, will profoundly alter our most cherished institutions. It will shatter our most deeply entrenched assumptions about how we should live our lives.

Everything nonmaterial will change. Things that have their basis in scientific facts and in empirically tested procedures will not, of course, be affected. Techniques for doing surgery, and engineering plans for building skyscrapers, will not be changed by the revolution I envision, nor will the legitimate use of medication for panic attacks, obsessive-compulsive disorders, and some cases of depression.

But how we "do" church, how we influence lives, how we provide social and moral leadership, how we live together in families and in communities, will radically be altered.

Celebrities will become obscure. A few sentences from an elder will mean more than all the secrets of effective living that are shared by an acclaimed communicator at a weekend seminar. Big "Christian" events will be limited to evangelism or to meaningful prayer, passionate worship, or biblical instruction. People will covet an evening in a mentor's home more than the chance to attend a motivational rally. They will know that the former has more life-changing power than the latter. Award banquets in the Christian community will feel less like Hollywood events. People will be honored in a way that meaningfully humbles them rather than holds them up as more significant because of their achievements. No one will compete with Christ for top honors.

In my dream, I see:

A GENERATION OF MENTORS, wise elders who are more valued than trained specialists in helping us respond to the challenges of life; godly men and women whose power and wisdom reach more deeply into our souls than an expert's knowledge and skill.

If my dream is to come true, it will require a miracle of God, not the splashy kind of pseudo-miracle that ignites a *movement* but the solid, deep variety that can begin a *reformation*. We've had plenty of movements, plenty of happenings that create huge followings and make it to the headlines. But we haven't had a reformation for quite a few years. Maybe it's time.

My dream boils down to a sentence as simple as it is profound: *If men become men, the world will change.* It is also true that if women become women, the world will change. A book could be written—and should be—about a parallel dream, a dream about older women who become mothers, and younger ones who learn to sister. Such a book about spiritual mothers and sisters would be a fitting companion to this book about spiritual fathers and brothers.

In my dream, older men will father and younger men will brother. When men throughout the world *recover their voice, release their power*, and *recapture the joy* in following God's call to become authentic men, the very nature of Christian community will change. That's my dream.

But I'm worried. I'm worried by the very things that should reassure me. I'm worried by the amount of attention this whole topic of manhood is receiving. I'm worried that whatever good that is developing will wash away in a coming backlash, when the men's movement will be exposed as a building on sand.

I'm worried that we are not facing up to the terrible problems within us that disfigure our manhood, problems that only painful and lengthy surgery can cure. I'm worried that we've set our sights too low, that we're running after something too easily achieved, that a deepened love for Christ is not at the center of things.

Maybe we're settling for a counterfeit of authentic manhood. I sometimes think that this idea of "becoming real men" has been reduced to a cultural fad, a mere *movement* accompanied by the usual elements: the excitement of big crowds, the hope of new formulas, the inspiration of challenging speakers, the determination of shouted commitments, and the ideas of current gurus.

What we do *not* need is a temporary burst of resolve and passion. What we *do* need is reformation, that deep work of God marked by repeated cycles of brokenness, repentance, perseverance, and joy. We need God's empowerment to enter the mystery of relationships at a level of life-giving connection that enthusiasm and slogans can never produce. We need to abandon ourselves to Christ in a way that releases all that his Spirit has placed within us.

We must spell out the cost of becoming men until the appeal of anything less is gone and only God's call remains.

If we are to become a generation of mentors and have a culture filled with men of character and wisdom, men that can lead the next generation into true godliness, then we must give careful thought to what men will look like when Christ is formed in them.

In a day when Satan's ability to sell us on a counterfeit of the real thing is at its peak, when we're likely to mistake a comfortably narrow path for the even narrower one, we must begin with a clear idea of what the miracle of manhood looks like.

---

1 *Oswald Chambers: Abandoned to God,* a biography by David McCasland (Grand Rapids: Discovery House Publishers, 1993), 74–75.

2 I do *not* believe that all personal problems are the direct result of personal, deliberate sin that more obedience can cure. See *Finding God* for a discussion of my views on this subject.

Chapter 2

Unmanly Men and Manly Men

This time he was in serious trouble. He had already offended enough important people to get himself in hot water. But never anything as bad as this.

His friends wanted to help. They were all young men, robust, determined, in the prime of life, eager to pursue what they believed in. They got together to discuss what they could do. None of their ideas would do much. And they knew it. Things were too far gone.

The conversation slowly shifted from ideas to complaints. They were mad. It just wasn't fair. Politics! That's all it was. Dirty, rotten politics.

Soon after the meeting, one of them, a swarthy, big man with olive skin weathered by many days at sea, tried to pick a fight with a flunky from the other side, thinking it would really feel good to hit someone. Even bad language gave some relief. But why wouldn't *he* do something? It was, after all, his battle, a battle for his neck.

Everyone was scared. All their hopes were crumbling. What would they do? What would happen to them if he were sent away? That was all they could think about.

Suddenly he called them together. Good! Now we're getting somewhere. He has a plan. He's ready to move, to take charge like a man. But all he said was, "Things are going to get pretty rough. And it's starting to get to me. I want you to stick close by." They had seen him troubled before. But not like this.

They wanted to stay involved with him. They really did. But it was hard to stand there helplessly and just watch. And they hadn't slept in days.

Why hadn't he spoken up at his hearing? He had friends in high places. Why didn't he call on them? He wasn't doing anything to help himself. He seemed resigned—no, *willing*—to endure terrible trouble as though it were his destiny.

He stayed so quiet, so calm, after that one time he fell apart. How did he manage to keep his cool and not scream for justice—or revenge? Through it all, right up to the end, he cared more about his friends—and his enemies—than about himself, even though he was the one facing his own worst nightmare.

Someone who had been watching him for some time put into words what many were thinking: "No man ever spoke like this one!"

This book is one small effort to encourage men to think hard about what it takes to become godly men, men who will be looked to by a few people in their community as elders, men who will be known more for their godly influence than for their talent or achievement.

Our culture is now divided into two groups of people: a few "significant" *experts*—trained theologians, popular pastors, influential business-men, skilled professionals, inspirational seminar leaders, self-help specialists, and comfortable middle-classers with steady jobs and beautiful kids, good folks who teach the "young marrieds class" at church—and *everybody else*, the ordinary people who go about their everyday business enjoying whatever pleasures they can find and enduring hard things as best they can. These are the people without thick cushions of money, comfort, and prestige to protect them from the tough questions and real pain—folks who wonder if what they experience is really all there is to life.

Imagine what it would be like if our Christian communities were made up not of experts and ordinary folks but of *elders* and *disciples*: elders, men and women who know God well (who would insist, of course, that they barely know him, but who would observably live to know him better); and disciples, vast throngs of people whose hearts have been stirred by the pos-sibility of actually knowing Christ, a possibility they see lived out in the lives of the truly mature. If reformation is to come, it will come through elders, not experts.

If ordinary men are to develop into fathers, if experts are to be changed into elders, we must develop some idea of what godly manhood looks like. We must get a picture of true masculinity that first will drive us to brokenness by making obvious our masculine failures and then will ignite a relentless passion to realize the staggering potential of becoming real men.

I therefore begin this chapter with a basic question: what does a godly man look like? (You can substitute the phrase "manly man" for "godly man." The two are the same.)

Is he broad-shouldered, self-confident, tough, successful? Is he powerful, committed to his purposes, able to keep in check emotions that might interfere with achieving his goals? Does he keep moving against all odds, never indulging the urge to panic or cry? Does his deepest enjoyment come more from what he has accomplished than from what he is like to be with?

That's the traditional view: real men are tough, tough enough to lead and make decisions and keep on moving. But for the last ten or twenty years, that view has taken a beating.

From pulpits, in conferences, and through books, modern men have been encouraged (sometimes commanded) to show their gentle side, to become comfortable with vulnerability and emotional displays, to stop thinking of themselves as superior to women, to release that part of their humanity that longs to *connect* more than *achieve*.

Men who live by God's design, so this thinking goes, are nicer, kinder, more considerate than we thought men were supposed to be. Aggression and power, those traditional "manly" qualities that have men out fighting the world while the ladies stay home, are now scorned as cultural mistakes, perversions of true masculinity.

In our modern understanding, whatever is legitimate about a "pioneering spirit" belongs as much to women as to men. And whatever is appealing about domestic life should draw both men and women back to home and hearth. No longer, we are told, should men hunt while women knit. Those stereotypes have more to do with a long history of patriarchal thinking than with Scripture. That's the view of many today.

But men have had a hard time putting down their bows and arrows and picking up needles and thread. The modern men's movement, now in full swing, arose partly as a reaction to the idea that men should become more relationally sensitive—more "feminized," as some have expressed it. Robert Bly got things going with his book *Iron John*, in which he wrote about a "wildness" inside all men that is waiting to move powerfully into life. In *Fire in the Belly*, Sam Keen added his rousing call to fan the fire in our bellies, to embrace and release our deepest passions.

Neither of these men, nor most subsequent leaders in the men's movement, want to return to a John Wayne style of masculinity (where men are more tough than tender), but they have expressed a legitimate concern that something primitive and basic about the nature of manhood is in danger of being lost in the culture's struggle to define it.

And I agree. Something has been lost. But exactly what is it? The idea of a primitive *wildness* struck a chord in men. The call to live out *passions* more basic than success and sex has been heard by thousands. When men stand together in huge Promise Keepers gatherings and *resolve* to honor their responsibilities, something deep in the hearts of men is released. And for that we should all be thankful.

Wildness, passion, determination—are these the core qualities of manhood that have been lost and are now being rediscovered?

For reasons presented in the rest of this book, I believe that the absolute center of manhood has been approached but not yet reached by what we have seen so far in the men's movement.

Something has been lost. Something is wrong with men. Something good that God has placed within every male—something that comes alive only through regeneration—remains unreleased in most men. For that reason few men are elders.

As a way of introducing our understanding of manhood, let me encourage you to think of masculinity as an *energy*, a natural momentum within the heart of every man, a power and an urge to move into life in a particular way.

Men in whom masculine energy is suppressed or distorted are unmanly, ungodly men, however culture may regard them. Men are manly only when they live in the power of released masculine energy. Now, what on earth does that mean?

To develop a clearer idea of what "released manhood" looks like, it might be helpful first to take a brief look at an *inauthentic man*, someone whose manly energy remains dormant or is expressed in corrupted form.

INAUTHENTIC MEN

If you are in relationship with an unmanly man, you likely will experience him as:

—*controlling* (impersonally powerful)
—*destructive* (or dangerous)

—*selfish* (committed, above all else, to feeling a certain way about himself)

An unmanly man *controls* conversations; he manipulates family and friends; he arranges his life to avoid whatever he is not sure he can handle. He trusts no one, not deeply. He works hard to maneuver himself into a favorable light, into a position where he comes out on top or at least unchallenged. He is not a good listener. He rarely asks meaningful questions, preferring either to offer opinions or remain quiet. No one feels pursued by him except when their friendship might work to his advantage. When he does take an interest in you, it has the feel of a car salesman asking to see a picture of your family.

And he is *destructive*. His words and actions harm people, though coworkers may feel encouraged and challenged for a time (sometimes a long time). Family members feel the harm soonest and most deeply but are sometimes too scared to admit it, even to themselves. Often the veneer of goodness and affability is so thick that the harm is felt only with a cumulative power that slowly destroys, like small traces of poison in drinking water. Sometimes he actively hurts people with sarcasm and meanness, occasionally with violence. More often the damage is done by indifference and retreat, the kind of weapons that make you feel guilty or weird for feeling attacked. The wife of an unmanly man rarely senses that she is cherished. She may never tell him so, but she more often feels used, taken for granted, or hated. His children and friends keep their distance. They're too angry, or scared, to get close.

His *selfishness* is not always apparent, but it reveals itself clearly in hard times. In spite of kindness and a generosity that is sometimes extravagant, a bottom-line commitment to his own well-being clearly surfaces when the chips are down.

Unmanly men are controlling, destructive, and selfish. But these traits describe only what is visible to others, what people feel in his presence. Scratch beneath the surface (sometimes a thick one) and you will discover that there is, supporting these weeds, a root system that has a stubborn life of its own. In depths that usually remain unexplored, unmanly men feel *powerless* beneath their determination to control; a hateful *rage* empowers their destructiveness; and they are *terrified* to a degree that makes selfishness seem their only hope for survival. Look inside an unmanly man and you will find a powerless, angry, terrified man trying to keep his life together through control, intimidation, and selfishness. The first three characteristics—controlling, intimidating, selfish—are typical of an unmanly man's style of relating, typical of how he comes across. The second three—powerless, angry, terrified—represent the battles going on deep inside his soul, beneath his style of relating. Let's take a closer look at this second set of characteristics, which represents what's going on inside an unmanly man.

Powerless

Brent had a history of backing away from women right at the point when the next step was commitment. He explained the pattern this way: "I'm just not sure if I have the right stuff to make a relationship work. What happens if she requires me to do something I can't do, or be someone I'm not?"

Men who feel powerless like things predictable. They don't enjoy surprises. The unexpected is a thrilling adventure only when it occurs in areas where an unmanly man feels specially competent. The adrenaline flows in a seasoned surgeon when something goes wrong on the table. He may later admit he was scared, but he does what needs to be done in the moment and he does it well.

Businessmen with a history of success sometimes display steel nerves and good judgment in crises that send "lesser" men quaking to their knees. Experienced plumbers with a knack for sniffing out what's wrong and knowing exactly what to do to fix it are bored by plugged drains and routine leaks. Bigger problems give them a chance to strut their stuff. Intellectuals rise to the challenge of debate. They welcome an opposing argument like a bull welcomes a red cape. It's a call to charge.

Whether surgeon, CEO, plumber, or intellectual, it's all the same. Uncertainty provides an exciting challenge to men only when it is in areas where they feel sure of their abilities.

But beneath the confidence of the most gifted man is a fear that won't diminish. Unmanly men are haunted by the possibility of something happening that they cannot handle, something that requires them to enter unfamiliar territory where their adequacy remains unproven, where their proven talents may be useless. Every honest man feels that fear. An unmanly man feels nothing more strongly than that fear but denies how strong it is within him.

Men who are otherwise strong may dread speaking to a Sunday school class, talking to their daughters about sex, picking the right restaurant for an anniversary celebration, or expressing their deepest sentiments to friends. It is no surprise that unmanly men feel most powerless in the one area that no one can effectively control—personal relationships. Getting close to their wives, feeling wise enough to be respected by their kids, building healthy intimacy with friends: these are the kinds of areas that have the power to make men feel impotent.

To hide their impotence, powerless men find something they can control—something they can handle well—and they avoid what they fear. They then regard whatever they can control as important and occupy most of their energy in handling it. It may be something as mundane as keeping a car clean, as wrong as seducing another woman, as irritating as lightening up every serious conversation with a joke, as well-received as writing a best-selling critique of culture, or as consuming as growing a business or expanding a ministry. Powerless men spend their lives controlling some outcome and deceiving themselves into thinking it matters.

Angry

Angry men are easily irritated. They are incensed when someone asks them to operate out of their sphere of competence, to use resources they aren't sure they have. When a wife asks for involvement, an angry man tends to think of what he already has given her. It's usually a list of material things ("Look at the house we live in"), uncommitted sins ("I've always been faithful to you"), or favorable comparisons with other men ("At least I'm not glued to the TV, watching sports every night like your brother. We go out to dinner with friends, I'm in church every Sunday, and I even drive Susie to her piano lessons. What more do you want?").

Unmanly men are easily provoked. Nothing big is required to ignite the outburst of an anger that is never far from the surface. Life itself continually demands that men do more than they feel capable of doing. Responsibilities never let up. Flossing your teeth today does not mean you can skip doing it again tomorrow. And even faithful flossing does not guarantee a good checkup.

When you do escape the dentist's office without hearing the drill, the joy is short-lived. A mole appears on your back, and it's a funny color. Or your teenage son brings home a bad report card. You wonder if he's lazy, on drugs, or bothered by attention deficit disorder. Maybe he needs those good drugs that make kids less distractible; maybe a private Christian school.

Then your air conditioner breaks just as summer hits. Your wife tells you she hasn't felt romanced for a long time. And you want to kill, hit, scream.

There are seasons of life when everything goes wrong. And there are seasons, usually shorter ones, when most things go right. Everyone's getting along, the IRS owes you a refund, and your daughter is dating the president of the youth group. But even during the good times, you're aware of a vague dread that feels threatening, like the one dark cloud hovering over your picnic.

"Give me a break!" we shout to no one in particular, or to God if we admit that our rage is directed toward him. And life (or God) seems to reply, "Get ready! The other shoe is going to drop. When? I want to surprise you."

It's enough to make someone mad. And anger, the kind most of us feel, reliably justifies actions that, to a nonangry mind, would instantly be recognized as wrong. The actions that seem right when we're angry damage others and make us feel better. We like both effects.

But the satisfaction is shallow and short-lived. It eventually yields to emptiness. And we feel less able to handle life's continuing demand to keep on moving.

At some point, we can think of nothing but revenge. The blatant urge to destroy doesn't become a fixed pattern in most men, but it boils up at odd moments and with fierce intensity. Unmanly men feel strangely good when they sense a power within themselves capable of destroying. They feel even better when they release it.

This release of corrupted masculine energy may take the form of sarcasm, of telling "in" jokes that purposefully exclude others, of using a sharp intellect to intimidate, of simple neglect. It may be experienced more violently, either in fantasy or through physical abuse.

When a man is not experiencing the joy that only released masculine energy can create, he is drawn to the pleasure of power. Destructive men are not manly: they are mad with the energy of distorted masculinity; they are mad at people and mad at life and mad at God. They are full of vengeful judgment toward everyone but themselves.

When I follow someone moving slowly down a flight of steps, sometimes the urge occurs to help them descend more quickly. The idea of pushing someone and watching them tumble down the stairs can be appealing.

Terrified

What if life exposes me as a failure, someone who cannot handle its legitimate demands? What if I am unable to deal effectively with matters that I must admit are truly important? What if I ruin everything—my family, my friendships, my job—and I am left alone, a loser standing naked for everyone to see? What if I face the fact that all my money, possessions, and good times haven't filled that awful emptiness deep inside?

Unmanly men live with a quiet terror that, like high blood pressure, slowly and silently kills. The terror won't go away. Usually it remains hidden under the wraps of success, sociability, and routine. Sometimes it erupts. And when it erupts, unmanly men panic or get depressed; sometimes they feel the urge to commit suicide, to kill someone else, or to enjoy the unique pleasures of immorality.

Whether the terror remains quiet or explodes into awareness, relief feels necessary. Whatever is required to find relief seems reasonable, entirely legitimate. But although the idea of beating up your dog or screaming at your wife has its appeal, arranging for instant, reliable pleasure feels better. It dulls the terror with a consuming enjoyment that involves no risk.

Options abound. Pornographic pleasure is as near as your local drugstore. If buying *Playboy* is over a line you still won't cross, similar pleasures are available within your imagination and memory. A visit to the restaurant where the well-shaped waitress—the one that always smiles at you—works the breakfast shift will help. The goal is RELIEF: quick, reliable, and easily arranged. Enjoying God is harder work. Terrified men want relief now!

Let me summarize. When masculine energy is not released, when it is either suppressed or distorted, men

1. feel powerless; they compensate by committing themselves to controlling something. They become AGGRESSIVE MEN.

2. experience rage and persuade themselves that vengeance is their due. They become ABUSIVE MEN.

3. live with a terror for which there is no resolution or escape, only relief. They dull the terror with physical pleasure and become ADDICTED MEN.

MANLY MEN

An authentic man is very different. When the energy God has placed within a man is released,

1. the man knows he is strong, not powerless. Strong men take the initiative, even when they're not sure what to do. Their calling to reflect God in their manner of relating compels them more than their hope for power or their fear of impotence. A manly man is not an aggressive man; he is an ACTIVE MAN, involved in offering quality relationships to others, more committed to developing a strength that others can enjoy than to achieving for himself a sense of power and control.

2. the man experiences a state of being less angry, less easily threatened. Some call it peace. For him the phrase "more than a conqueror" means something, even during life's hard moments. A manly man's pain doesn't interfere with his feeling the plight of others, even when their troubles are less severe than his. He has the courage to face his experience honestly. He therefore feels the sadness of living in a fallen world, and the loneliness of living in imperfect community.

But his sadness and loneliness generate only a righteous anger, the kind that stirs compassion for people, while it remains offended by sin. A released man is not abusive; he is a GENTLE MAN, not weak, a man whose power is controlled for good purposes.

3. the man finds an answer to his terror: in FREEDOM. No matter what happens in life, manly men always find room to move. There is always something to BE, even when there is nothing to DO.

When their families fall apart or their businesses collapse, manly men—like unmanly men—are tempted to lash out in vengeance or to retreat into relief.

But they do neither. They are drawn by the opportunity to exhibit something good, to reflect the always hopeful movement of God. They move through trials with a presence that others, more than they, notice.

Manly men are enticed by the joys of freedom, by the unhindered chance to follow the call of manhood. A manly man is not addicted; he treats his body roughly, to avoid coming under a foreign power. He fights hard against his relentless desire for pleasure. He moves according to a plan. He is a PURPOSEFUL MAN who knows what he's about and what he can contribute to the purpose for which he is living.

Every day, we move either toward godly manhood or away from it.

One of the great tragedies of our day is that so many men are walking a path that they think leads to the joys of legitimate masculinity. It may be many years before those moving in wrong directions realize that the path they have been following releases masculine energy that is more corrupt than genuine, and that this path leaves them even more powerless, bitter, and terrified.

"There is a way that seems right to a man, but in the end it leads to death" (Proverbs 14:12).

Before I discuss the essence of true masculinity, I want to think about the deep passion in men that keeps them walking the path away from godly manhood.

Chapter 3

Recipe Theology

Both of them were nervous—and mad. It was their first session with Dr. Gilbert, the marriage counselor their pastor had recommended. Toward the end of their first year of marriage, she had started talking about getting help. He never liked the idea. He thought they could work things out on their own. If she hadn't threatened to leave, he would not be sitting in Dr. Gilbert's office now, two weeks shy of their second anniversary. He was twenty-nine. She was a year younger.

She looked nervous. He was pretty sure he didn't. "Look, I'll go to one session," he had told her, "to see if this guy knows what he's talking about."

After offering coffee, which they both declined, Dr. Gilbert opened the conversation rather directly. "Tell me what brought you here." No nonsense, the young man thought. That was good. Kind, but to the point.

She needed no wider door to storm through, and she started with words her husband had heard before. "Dr. Gilbert, our marriage is really in trouble."

For nearly fifteen minutes, she lashed out at him with one story after another. An up-and-down courtship, then a marriage all down. Nearly constant fighting. No real intimacy. None. Just sex. Can't endure it much longer. Didn't get married for this.

She wrapped up the attack with her most familiar complaint: "Whenever I try to tell him how I feel, he either lectures me on how I'm wrong or he just says nothing."

Her husband decided to speak up. No invitation from Dr. Gilbert was necessary. "Listen, I've told her a million times that I'm willing to do whatever it takes to make our marriage work. I love her. I even went with her to some seminar that she thought might help. And I really tried to do what the guy said. Lots of stuff about communicating better, telling her I love her in ways she can hear, following some steps that the guy said would put a spark back in our relationship."

He paused to study the counselor's face. Dr. Gilbert looked neither convinced nor skeptical.

The young man continued. "Our pastor told my wife that you were pretty good, so I agreed to give it a try. She's right about one thing. We really don't get along. I figured if I had a toothache, I'd see a dentist; so if my marriage needs fixing, I guess it makes sense to see a counselor."

She nearly came out of her chair. "Do you see what he's like?" she thundered. "I want a man to *relate* to me, so we can share our lives together. He wants to fix something broken. He makes our marriage sound like a broken car."

Then, more quietly, with tears, she continued. "I'm not a thing that's broken. I'm a person, a woman, who just wants to be loved. I just don't know if we'll ever be happy together." The tears flowed freely.

He hated it when she cried. It always made something tighten inside him. He felt helpless. Angry, scared too, but more helpless than anything else. She kept crying. He sat motionless.

Dr. Gilbert broke the silence. "Tell me what's going through your mind right now."

The question was directed to him. He could only shrug his shoulders and say, "I don't know what to do."

When I was a boy, I often would lie on my back in the warm grass of summer, just before bedtime, and stare into the star-filled sky. I remember feeling small—and I remember liking that feeling; I think it was because I knew there was something big into which I fit, something far bigger than me. I didn't know what that something was, but I knew it had to do with a big story that God was telling. I wanted to know that story, and I wanted to be a part of it.

I have since discovered that gazing into the sky is a very different experience from studying in a library, writing a doctoral dissertation, or counseling in a professional office. Stargazing lets me ponder the big picture. The other activities tend to absorb me in smaller details. My adult responsibilities have mostly been driven by the need to figure things out—to understand, for example, why some men feel homosexual urges, while others struggle with depression—and to know how to overcome problems. That's what a psychologist is supposed to do: figure out what's wrong and fix it.

And that's what today's Bible teachers and pastors and other Christian leaders are expected to do, as well: become experts in handling the "real" problems of life. If they're successful, they become known as competent people. If not, they're exposed as weak, or dismissed as not terribly useful. Either way, Christian leaders and helpers seem more interested in the bits and pieces of life than in the big picture, the one I saw painted in the sky, where the glory of God is declared and the work of his hands is proclaimed (Psalms 19:1).

As a result, the theological statements coming out of modern culture look more like recipes for living than declared truths about God. *Transcendent theology*, which flows out of the big picture, has been replaced by *recipe theology*, a way of thinking that keeps its focus on the particulars of life. The center of transcendent theology is God, his character and purpose. The center of recipe theology is man, his needs and well-being.

That kind of thinking affects the way we approach our everyday lives. Take our example at the opening of this chapter, the story of a husband governed by two bits-and-pieces assumptions: (1) someone knows what he should do to resolve his particular marital crisis, and (2) if he finds that someone and follows his or her advice, his marriage will improve. The seminar leader wasn't the right expert. Perhaps the counselor will have the recipe that can make the marriage work.

Most of us naturally think that way. We want to believe that someone knows exactly what we should do to fix our problems, and—depending on how bad our problems are—we're willing to do whatever that someone suggests. We have become a culture of EXPERTS and FOLLOWERS, all determined to figure out the bits and pieces of life.

Listen to a few examples of recipe thinking:

—"Do you want to know how to recover from the damage sustained in your childhood? Here are the ingredients God provides. Mix them according to this plan and you'll whip up a delicious meal of personal worth."

—"Perhaps you need to make a job decision, or better handle the stress in the job you already have. Here are a couple of biblical principles to guide you. Apply them to your life and you'll soon find the confidence to move ahead and the joy of knowing you're in the center of God's will."

—"Are you angry? Can't get close to your mate or resolve tensions with a friend? Here's God's prescription for getting rid of your anger, resolving tension, and building intimacy. And remember: HIS medicine always works."

This bits-and-pieces approach to life affects how a man—whether godly or ungodly—views himself. A man feels least like a man when he feels forced by circumstances to throw up his hands and admit, "I have no idea what to do," and then does nothing. Indecisive husbands or boyfriends, pleasant cowards, whining victims: these are visibly weak men. They live their lives sitting still. Like a flag hanging limp on a windless day, these men don't move except to do such "manly" things as yelling at women or smaller men, drinking too much, or masturbating to favorite fantasies. In a culture that expects men to know what to do, it's tough to face a problem that has no recipe for solution.

Men often report feeling most like men when they can say "I may not know what to do about THIS, but I know what to do about THAT. I know I can do it, I'm doing it, and it's working." These men may be successful businessmen but distant fathers. Because they live within the boundaries of their competence, they are usually not aware of any struggle with their sense of manhood. They face only those problems that they are pretty sure they can handle.

Men who feel like men are not necessarily manly. Men who feel like men because of their competence rarely notice that areas they call THIS—those things they aren't sure how to handle—involve their most significant relationships, and areas they call THAT—those things they manage well—have more to do with non-relational tasks they feel comfortable doing. Men who, for their sense of well-being, depend on facing tasks they can handle are not usually effective in their close relationships.

Often they refuse to let their wives express how lonely, hurt, and misunderstood they feel. Whatever concerns they do hear they either fix or ignore. These men take their sons to ball games but never take them for long walks. And they don't reveal their struggles to anyone, especially not their sons. Competent men neither listen well nor share openly.

They may have good times with their daughters—lots of laughing, good-natured teasing, and angry promises to protect ("If any boy hurts you, I'll punch his lights out")—but they have few conversations with them; they don't know much about intimate, two-way talks.

Because they have no opportunity to relax in goodness deep enough to absorb their badness, no chance to rest in a strong love that can be trusted to endure, wives and daughters of competent men have a hard time going off duty. They have to keep things together. Competent men breed tough women.

I suggest that a man is most manly when he admits "I don't know what to do in this situation, but I know it's important that I get involved and do something. I will therefore envision what God may want to see happen in this person's life or in this circumstance, and I will move toward that vision with whatever wisdom and power God supplies me." A manly man moves even when there are no recipes.

My quarrel with recipe theology is not with the biblical principles it affirms or with its requirement that we follow them. It is rather with its tendency to make biblical principles into a formula for success.

God has not written a cookbook for living, with recipes for every dish we may want to prepare. He responds to our individual situations by inviting us to participate in a story larger than our lives. Recipe theology studies the bits and pieces of life in order to help us tell *our* story better. God invites us to join him in telling *his*.

I wonder if the central passion that rules our culture today is the passion to make life work. We think it should work: if not life in general, then certainly *our* lives at any given moment. We should feel good about ourselves, enjoy friendships, make a decent living, find a doctor who can cure us, and receive respect from our peers. Experts exist to help us make life work. So does God. When experts decide to call in God for help, they become recipe theologians.

We are so shortsighted.

Why? Why are we drawn to small-picture living and uninspired by the chance to be lifted up into the bigger picture that God is drawing? Why is it so hard to even challenge the "Life is supposed to work" assumption, let alone give up our demand that someone tell us how to manage it well? Why is recipe theology so popular?

Could it be that, like every generation before us, we've managed to shove at least one vital point of biblical truth into the background and have therefore developed a distorted view of Christianity and the Christian life?

OF ADAM

In Martin Luther's day, the church had lost sight of the doctrine of grace. The result was a recipe theology of indulgence and good works.

I wonder if we have, in our day, lost the excitement and drama of our calling: to reveal the unseen God by the way we live, especially by the way we relate to one another. The single most important truth about people is the truth most easily ignored: that we bear the image of God. As image-bearers, we are called to tell his story with our lives, not to tell our stories with his resources.

By neglecting that truth, the calling to be like God has been reduced to a whisper, and the invitation to make our lives work better is being given with a shout. We tend to be either recovery addicts ("How can I *feel* better?") or grim legalists ("How can I *do* better?"). The truth about revealing God to others through our lives has been reduced to religious rhetoric that receives our token assent. Meanwhile we go about the "real" work of getting our lives together and making ourselves comfortable. We prefer practical help over a higher call to live by design.

The difficulty, of course, is this: we will never handle our problems well, nor fulfill our responsibilities with spiritual motivation, until first we honor the call to bear God's image, and determine to know him well. Begin with recipe theology and you never rise beyond yourself. Begin with transcendent theology and you end up becoming the self you were designed to be.

Let me explain. The two biggest topics within recipe theology today are *solving problems* (the call to healing) and *fulfilling responsibilities* (the call to obedience).

Either we become preoccupied with feeling good or we feel pressured to do good. Neither lifts us up into God's larger story or invites us to participate in it.

Those who think that nothing matters more than relieving the pain of a badly damaged identity, or learning to be valued and accepted in a loving relationship, will be drawn to the bits and pieces of a recipe theology for recovery. They will look for an expert who can guide them toward a fuller, freer, happier experience of themselves in a difficult world. Commitment to duty may be strongly encouraged, but if push comes to shove, finding happiness will take priority over keeping promises.

A counselee once told me, "I feel so much better about myself as a man when I am with the other woman. I know it's wrong, but I just can't imagine that God wants me to stay with my wife if we make each other so miserable."

Experts on the other end, those who specialize in firm exhortation, think less of enjoying God as "Abba" and more of obeying him as a sergeant. Their emphasis finds expression in a very different theology: still a recipe, but with a systematic focus on the bits and pieces of responsibility. The effect is smugness, more self-righteousness than joy, and more pressure than freedom.

A friend told me that he once went to a counselor who in the first session gave him a computer printout of Bible verses and instructed him to memorize and obey each one. When people try to handle their lives by merely working hard to do better, they either fail and live in defeat or succeed and become proud.

Both errors leave us in a sphere of life we think we can manage. We like to think that there are steps we can follow for healing or that our duties to God can be laid out before us as a well-lit path we can walk along. Then things seem clear. We know what to do. We never have to leave the sphere of manageability. And we therefore never learn the dependence and trust that only grows in the darkness.

But think about what would happen if we found the courage to move beyond the manageable tasks of life and to enter the sphere of mystery, where there are no practical answers, where the courage to enter chaos is more necessary than the discipline to follow steps or rules. Suppose an angry father who had been focused only on finding a cure for his temper could feel caught up with the opportunity to introduce his son to the heart of God. He might not know exactly what to do, but the energy flowing out from him toward his son would be different.

If we could push the recipes off center stage, maybe the good principles they teach could again be seen as ways to know and reflect God, rather than as techniques to promote inner healing or as requirements to mechanically obey. Maybe then the character and purposes of God would regain their rightful place in our thinking and lead to the development of a transcendent theology.

The beginning point for understanding manhood and for being transformed into spiritual, manly men is not a recipe for developing masculinity nor a list of ingredients to stir together. We must begin with God's unique call to men. How have men been designed to be like God in ways that women have not? What is our special transcendent call?

Encouraging men to release those deeply masculine capacities that first existed in God and were then built into men, and helping men to reflect those characteristics of God that men can best reflect, require the wisdom of someone who has a feel for who God is and what he's up to. This demands a transcendent theologian. The expertise of a recipe theologian simply won't do.

Recipe theology fits better in what I call the SPHERE OF MANAGEMENT. Transcendent theology is required if we are to move about in the SPHERE OF MYSTERY. All of life can be divided into one of these two spheres.

Men naturally insist on operating within the sphere of management. Men who are on the road to authentic manhood find the courage to enter the sphere of mystery.

Let me define my terms:

> THE SPHERE OF MANAGEMENT exists wherever things are more or less predictable, where there is an order that can be understood well enough so that we can use it to make our lives work as we want.
> THE SPHERE OF MYSTERY exists wherever we are dealing with things that are finally unpredictable, where whatever order exists cannot be understood well enough to give us the control we desire.

In the sphere of management, we can move with the confidence that we have at least some power to control things, to set objectives and pursue them according to a workable plan. In the sphere of mystery, we can move only with a confidence in someone we trust but can never control. Whatever objectives belong in this sphere become matters for prayer, while our energy is devoted to pleasing God, not making something happen.

The tendency of our culture is to define relationships, including our relationship with God, as a task and then to figure out how to go about making them work. We like to think that growing in Christ, and developing strong relationships, belong in the sphere of management. So we put them there and try to figure out what to do. Men prefer to do something they can manage. And recipe theology lights the way.

We must return to a transcendent theology that empowers us to move into the darkness, where God does his deepest work. We must learn what it means to abandon ourselves to God, and to powerfully relate to others. And that will require that we enter the dark sphere of mystery.

Chapter 4

Entering Darkness

The tears welling up this time were different. More desperate. Not like the petulant tears that sometimes erupted when he didn't feel taken into account properly. And not at all like the pouty tears that made him feel like a demanding child not getting his way.

These tears were different. They felt cleaner, beyond hurt and sulkiness, not the sort that left streams of self-loathing in their wake.

He hurried off to be alone, wanting her to follow but not feeling weak for so wanting, knowing that neither she nor anyone else could give enough comfort to dry his tears. For one awful moment—as he stood by the railing, overlooking the lake—he could see into the black hole, the one he always knew was there but which he had never before seen, at least not so clearly.

The serene beauty of the unrippled blue water reflecting the jagged, snowcapped peaks of the Canadian Rockies provided a dramatic contrast to the writhing agony in his soul, where there was nothing but darkness: no answers, no beauty, no power, no meaning, no love. He was unnerved to the depths of his being—and it was all triggered by a moment of misunderstanding with his wife. That moment now felt like an innocent doorway that, once opened, had sucked him into the darkness of blackness.

The terror rose slowly upward, like a bad piece of food, until it shot out of his mouth with unchosen force: *"I don't know what to do!"* The shout was directed at no one—unless toward God, if he happened to be listening.

He heard no reply, no reassuring whisper; there was no comforting presence. The loneliness felt even more severe. Was this a taste of hell? Unending pain. No one to help. Absolute isolation.

But he wasn't in hell. The lake in front of him had undeniable beauty. His wife was next to him, gentle concern flowing freely from her burdened heart. And he knew he was in the presence of God: the hidden, silent God who was unmistakably there.

Strange, he thought. How desperate humility can feel. To be utterly dependent because one is fully undone.

That thought felt alive. It appeared from nowhere.

But still no comfort. The darkness was thick enough to feel. He couldn't move. Turn to his wife and apologize? But his greater guilt (though he couldn't yet put words to it) was against God. Give her a hug? But only a loved person can truly love another. Rehash the conflict? Pointless. Merely another opportunity to display his selfishness.

"I don't know what to do!" The shout came again. Nothing made sense. His guilt and coldness and selfishness made him feel trapped. Paralyzed.

"Will someone who knows please tell me what I am to do?"

Suddenly the question felt lifeless. It lost all its interest. He knew that there would be no answer, that demanding one was futile. Another path opened up to him. Something more troubling than his ignorance needed attention.

And then he heard something. Words coming from his own mind, new ones, unplanned, unbidden but entirely welcome. The darkness had blinded him—he still could not see—and what he now heard in the dark, he had never heard in the light.

"I really am in the darkness," he listened to himself say. "I don't know what to do. I am completely confused, utterly bewildered, and profoundly afraid. I feel shut up to God. This spot I am in reduces me to two choices: either wait till this mood passes and just get on with things as best I can, or abandon myself to God.

"It's no use just getting on. The darkness always returns, each time more horribly, to confront me again with the stupid choice I have made and to drive me in despair to the other one. The darkness—this terrible, benevolent angel—is making it all clear. There is nothing to do but trust!

"Oh God, with all my heart I abandon myself to you. Burn away the flesh. Fill me with your Spirit. You are more than worthy of my complete trust. Thank you for the darkness that stilled me enough to hear your voice."

He took his wife's hand and slowly walked back to their room. They still were not close. Neither felt what they both longed to feel. Honeymoon joy did not set in.

But he sensed that something far better lay ahead. And with that conviction, he felt himself wanting to move toward God, toward her, toward life, as he had never moved before. His wife felt the stirring of hope.

Men are called to move into darkness, to keep moving ahead with purpose and strength even when they cannot clearly see the path before them. Three observations from the record of creation in Genesis will help us see that God has already done what he calls men to do.

Observation #1

The first thing revealed about God in the Bible is that he is the CREATOR and that he created by SPEAKING INTO DARKNESS. This observation is discussed in Chapters 4 and 5.

Observation #2

The first thing revealed about man in the Bible is suggested by the Hebrew word, in Genesis 1:27, that is translated into English as *MALE*. Chapter 6 reflects on the significance of this word.

Observation #3

The first thing God told Adam to do was NAME THE ANIMALS. Adam was called to "speak order into existence" where there was none, just as God had done in creation. When Adam spoke, there was order. When he was silent, chaos returned. The implications of Adam's speaking and silence are thought through in Chapter 7.

We have seen what happens when men follow our culture into unmanliness. Finding solutions by using recipe theology has given us a bits-and-pieces approach to life, an approach that finds the opposite of true manhood and leads us away from mystery and faith. Now follow our thinking a bit further. Man, like God, was meant to speak into darkness and to become a storyteller.

After Jesus' death, two men were walking toward the village of Emmaus, sharing their disappointment and confusion over the events of the last few days. They didn't understand. But they thought about it as they kept walking. The Bible says, "They were talking with each other about everything that had happened. . . . They talked and discussed these things" (Luke 24:14–15).

Perhaps they *wanted* to understand.

Jesus (whom they did not recognize but whom they took for a stranger) joined them on their walk and asked them what they were talking about. They were surprised he had to ask and thought he must be from out of town. What else was there to discuss? The events surrounding the death of Jesus, and all that had happened in the past week, were so bewildering they could think of nothing else. All hope was gone. Nothing made sense. It was all a mystery: a confusing, unwelcome, dark mystery.

Jesus listened to them speak for a few minutes. And then—standing still, with an authority that made them stop—he looked at them sternly and said: "How foolish you are, and how slow of heart to believe all that the prophets have spoken! Did not the Christ have to suffer these things and then enter his glory?" (Luke 24:25–26).

He resumed walking, and as they followed, they listened to a Bible study led by the author. He began "with Moses and all the Prophets," and "he explained to them what was said in all the Scriptures concerning himself" (Luke 24:27). They later reported that their hearts burned with excitement as they listened to him reveal the Christ.

When we open our Bibles to the very beginning (as Jesus might have done with his two walking companions), the first thing we learn is that God is the creator of everything. The second thing we learn is that he did all his initial creating in the dark.

Listen to the first two sentences in the Bible: "In the beginning God created the heavens and the earth." Sentence one. "Now the earth was formless and empty, darkness was over the surface of the deep, and the Spirit of God was hovering over the waters." Sentence two.

The rest of Genesis 1 informs us that God spoke into that unshaped, naked darkness. He moved into that primordial *sphere of mystery* with imaginative power that brought beauty and life out of the confusion.

Ten times he spoke: the first four times, God gave shape to an unformed world; he established *order* (Genesis 1:3, 6, 9, 11). The next four times, God filled the emptiness with the *beauty of life* (Genesis 1:14, 20, 24, 26). The final two times, God revealed his heart toward the people he created, by *blessing* them with meaningful work to honor their dignity (Genesis 1:28) and with generous provision for their physical needs (Genesis 1:29–30). He had already given them himself and each other; they had no further personal needs.

Now pause for a moment. Is there something in this account that speaks of Christ? Paul told us that Christ was the one who made everything (Colossians 1:16). Christ was the one who spoke into darkness to bring order and beauty out of chaos.

What might the Creator have said to his two friends on the road to Emmaus when he talked about the ten times, so long ago, that he entered the mystery of dark-covered water in order to create life? What could he have made known about himself that had the power to change these two men into elders?

In the beginning, before Christ spoke, there was nothing but water: untamed, cold, lifeless water that was covered with an impenetrable blanket of darkness. It is important that we remember that God spoke into this darkness in order to create life. Peter implies that there is a connection between *forgetting how God created the world* and *becoming godless people.*

Listen to his words: "In the last days scoffers will come, scoffing and following their own evil desires. . . . They deliberately forget that long ago by God's word the heavens existed and the earth was formed out of water and by water" (2 Peter 3:3, 5).

Apparently, if we forget that God created by speaking into darkness, we are in danger of becoming ungodly. How? Why? What does this mean? At first glance the two seem unrelated.

But the connection between our remembering that God spoke into darkness and our becoming godly begins to become clear when we understand what the darkness was into which God spoke. In the next few chapters, we will suggest that men are called to move wisely into the darkest regions of their worlds; they are to speak powerful words into the confusion of life with the same energy that flowed out of Christ when he spoke into darkness (Colossians 1:16, 29).

THE MEANING OF DARKNESS

The Bible talks about several different kinds of darkness. There is the darkness of SECRECY, or wickedness, a darkness loved by people whose deeds are evil (John 3:19). Christians have been called out of this darkness into the light of full exposure and full forgiveness (1 Peter 2:9). The shadowy shroud of darkness of this type, like the streets of Dickens' London, keeps evil deeds out of sight. It has no place in the nature of God. In him there is no darkness, no region kept secret to avoid exposure of a flaw (1 John 1:5).

Jude refers to a related concept when he tells us that rebellious angels are "kept in darkness, bound with everlasting chains for judgment on the great Day" (Jude 6). This is the darkness of JUDGMENT, the terrible thing that happens when God, who is light, withdraws himself completely.

But there is a third kind of darkness mentioned in Scripture. It is the darkness that covered the water into which God spoke when he created life. This darkness has more to do with disorder and random chaos than with either hidden wickedness or punishment for evil.

It is a darkness over which the Spirit of God *hovered* in the opening scene of Scripture, suggesting an expectancy that something was about to happen. This is the darkness of CONFUSION, randomness that is about to yield to the light of order and beauty, a pointless chaos with utterly no shape and no spark of life, but still a chaos that could be transformed into something wonderful.

The darkness of confusion is so thick that it stops all natural movement. When God covered Egypt with darkness (the same word in Genesis 1:2 is used in Exodus 10:21–22), it was a darkness that could be felt. No one moved for three days.

When the tour guide turns out the lights in an underground cavern, there is no need to tell people to stand still. In darkness that completely eliminates sight, no one moves.

When God gave the law at Mount Sinai, the mountain was surrounded by "black clouds and deep darkness" (Deuteronomy 4:11, same word again). The people, we're told, "heard the sound of words but saw no form; there was only a voice" (Deuteronomy 4:12).

In the darkness of confusion, you cannot see but you can hear; at least, you can hear the voice of God. Natural movement, the kind that depends on sight, completely stops in darkness. But supernatural movement, both the movement of God and the movement of a man who walks by faith rather than sight, is possible even in the darkest darkness.

When the curtain lifts and the biblical drama begins, we immediately see Christ at center stage. The story opens with God confronting the original sphere of mystery: the darkness covering unformed, unfilled waters. There was no design, no order, no beauty, no life—just darkness.

The Spirit hovers about the darkness. Then God speaks. With power greater than darkness, he moves into mystery and gives life through his word.

Now notice something filled with significance for our study of manhood. The first thing God told the man to do was *name the animals*, creatures that God could have named but didn't. "He brought them to the man to see what he would name them; and whatever the man called each living creature, that was its name" (Genesis 2:19). God gave the responsibility to name the animals to the man, not to the woman. Eve was not yet created.

Like God, man was called to speak into darkness, to move into the confusion of a completely unnamed kingdom of animals, and to assign every one a name. In ancient Near Eastern culture, to name something implied the authority to define its character, to give shape to its nature, to fill a void with something that came out of the one who gave the name.

Could it be that God intended men to behave like him by courageously moving into whatever spheres of mystery they encounter and speaking with imagination and life-giving power into the confusion they face?

Since the fall from grace, every man's life is filled with confusion. Consider just a few examples. What should a man do when his wife demeans him in front of friends? Should he

—rebuke her?
—ignore it?
—say something kind?
—bring it up later, telling her how she made him feel?
—never bring it up?

What should a man do when he hates his job? Should he

—quit complaining and be grateful he gets a paycheck?
—look for other work?
—accept the job as a gift from God?
—figure out what he most dislikes and see if anything can be changed?

What should a man do when there is conflict with a close friend? Should he

   —talk to his friend about it, in the spirit of Matthew 18:15–17?

   —overlook it with a love that covers a multitude of sins?

   —bring his friend's faults to his attention in an effort to promote growth?

Masculinity begins to grow when a man asks questions for which he knows there are no answers.

No man can escape the sphere of mystery. If he lives in relationship and has any desire at all for the relationship to work, he will face unsolvable confusion. If a man is to be fully a man, he must learn what it means to move in darkness. And that will require him to admit "I don't know what to do" with a despair so real that no recipe will help.

Recipes are useful in a well-lighted kitchen. Recipe theology, that collection of practical biblical principles that tell us what to do in every situation, treats confusion as something to be solved rather than entered. It reduces the mysteries of life to things we can manage.

Recipe theologians tell us how to make life work by simplifying things and relieving confusion. Transcendent theologians know there is a darkness of confusion that can only be entered by knowing Christ, by abiding in him, by trusting him to supply supernatural power to hover over whatever darkness we face, and then by moving into that darkness with words that bring life.

Once there is a commitment to go into darkness and mystery, a man must move forward, determined to tell a good story and to not be silent. My cowriters, Don Hudson and Al Andrews, speak to these matters next. In Chapter 5, Don writes about the one story that we men must tell as we journey on: the story of God. That story reminds us that we can make it, that we can keep on going. In Chapter 6, Al calls us to remember our own stories of how God worked in our lives—stories that bring hope, even more when they are shared in community. And in Chapter 7, Don shows us that to act like God when we are in the darkness, to honor our calling to make him known, is to break our silence and speak. And thus to become men.

Chapter 5

From Chaos to Chaos

The ringing of the phone splintered the night in two. It took a second ring to rouse him out of a deep sleep. The third ring made him conscious of his surroundings. He looked at the clock. It was two in the morning. *Who in the world would be calling at this time of night?* he asked himself. He reached for the phone in what felt like slow motion. Just as his hand gripped the receiver, he hesitated. *Either this is a prank call or something serious is wrong. I hope it's a prank call*, he told himself. The fourth ring. He jerked the receiver off the carriage and put it to his ear.

Someone wept softly on the other end of the line. After a few unbearable seconds, she spoke hesitantly. "Son. This is your mom. Your father has had an emergency."

His mother's words numbed him into disbelief. He tried to convince himself. *My father is only sixty-four. He's too young for anything life-threatening.*

"What's wrong?" the young man asked.

"He had a heart attack while he was getting ready for bed," she explained. "I called 911 and then gave him CPR. We're in the emergency room now and he's with the doctors." Then her tone of voice changed. He knew this tone too well. And he hated it, because she would speak to him as if he were still a boy.

"Now, son. Don't you worry. We're fine, and everything is going to be okay," she intoned with a deadpan voice.

He ignored her statement and said he would be on the next plane out. She argued halfheartedly, explaining that it would be a wasted trip. He hung up the phone.

Images of his father and himself drifted through his mind. Wrestling on the floor. Fishing the waters of the Smokies. Watching his father cry one time in his life: at *his* father's funeral. Sleeping close to his father, as a small boy, in the hunting cabin one night. He lingered on this particular image.

It was when he was six years old. A bobcat screamed outside the window. Within a second, he was out of his bed and in his father's bed, under the covers and jammed up against him. It was a safe world beside his father. What would he do without him?

Enough of this, he lectured himself. *I have much too much to do. And Dad may pull through.*

His older brother met him at the airport when he reached his destination. He knew as soon as he saw his brother's face. His words were unnecessary.

"Dad's dead. He died two hours ago. Massive heart attack."

His brother turned on his heels and walked toward the baggage claim. He called over his shoulder, "We have a lot to do."

Once again the feeling of slow motion entered his life. He obediently followed his older brother while trying to swallow the awful truth.

Standing on the moving sidewalk, he began to feel his first emotions. He watched people pass him. *They don't know. If they had any idea that my father was dead, they would stop. They would turn around and go home. If they knew that my father was dead, they would understand that their lives no longer make sense. The world should stop spinning on its axis. Life should be over. Why would God take him now? My two-year-old son loves him so much. What will I tell him? He won't understand. I wish I could talk to my father. I wish I could pick up the phone and ask him what to do with this one. He would know. But he's gone.*

He became angrier as the thoughts flooded his mind. By the time he and his brother reached the car, he was furious. Not sad, just furious.

The week of his father's funeral was an unbearable nightmare for the young man. Well-meaning people invaded the house. Some family members handled themselves poorly. No one could say the right words. Because he was an intensely private man, every person's presence felt like an intrusion to his grief.

His son asked incessantly, "Where's Grandpa?" No question brought more despair than this one. It seemed that every thirty minutes he was trying to find words to explain that Grandpa was in heaven. "Will he be right back?" his son would ask with searching eyes.

"No, son. He's not coming back."

He could not look in his wife's eyes. Occasionally he would give her an obligatory hug. He would not let her comfort him. He ignored his mother as kindly as possible.

The day after the funeral he disappeared. Not physically. He was there, but he was a shell of a man. In the morning, he took care of small details with the funeral home, studied his father's life insurance policy, and paid outstanding bills. That afternoon, as he sat on the back porch of his parents' home, he was obsessed with a few things that made him feel alive, like anger.

He was angry. This emotion he knew well. He always felt angry, although very few people knew it. But this was more than anger. He felt violent. His wife came onto the porch and asked him if he'd like to take a walk with her. He looked at her with disgust and said, "In the heat of the day?"

"We can wait for it to get cooler," she said. He ignored her words and turned away. She felt alone as he picked up a magazine and idly flipped through the pages.

He felt particularly violent when anyone moved toward him with kindness. He wanted to harm anyone who got close to him. Life had handed him a tragic blow. Someone should pay for the injustice. His anger was a quiet coldness that pushed everyone away.

But he could not endure such intense rage for long. Eventually his anger did nothing more than remind him that he was helpless—that he was powerless in the face of this tragedy. He wanted something that would help him disappear or relieve his pain. Something that would help him forget.

So he fantasized. He dreamed of other women. He abandoned himself to lustful thoughts. Drawing near to his wife at a time like this was out of the question. He idled away the afternoon, living in his unbridled fantasies.

He sat until sunset, and in the cool of the evening, he remembered that he had next Sunday's sermon to prepare.

Sex and violence—topics that stir every man. The movie and book industries generate billions of dollars from these two topics alone. Men know the power of anger. Men understand the allure of sex.

When faced with the worst chaos of his life, the man in this story found comfort in anger and sexual fantasy. He was enraged that his father was taken from him so soon. Most of his friends' fathers were older than his, and yet they were still alive. Why was his father dead?

At that time in his life, memories of his father failed to relieve his pain. In fact, they haunted him. They were nothing more than a reminder of the good man who was gone. To escape the pain of his father's death, he lost himself in sexual fantasies. He no longer felt the comfort of having a father to ask for advice. He was angry that he was alone. Chaos—that confusing darkness that enters everyone's world—intruded into this man's world, and he turned to something that helped, something that felt natural.

How do men typically respond to the chaos of their lives?

Recall the temptation story. In the beginning, in the Garden of Eden, Adam did not know that chaos existed. The creation story in Genesis began with chaos but ended with creation. "And God saw that what he made was good." He transformed the wasteland into a paradise and gave it to Adam and Eve for their home. Before Adam's disobedience, the man succeeded in every endeavor. There were no thorns and thistles. His work, rather than being a frustration, gave him ultimate satisfaction. And more importantly, he enjoyed perfect relationships with his wife and with his God.

Then chaos reentered the story. In the culture of the time Genesis was written, the serpent was a symbol of chaos, of an unmanageable darkness. The serpent confused God's word by questioning Eve about God's wisdom. He darkened the clarity of God's truth. Darkness, once again, hovered over the earth. A later chapter in this book explains how Adam chose silence when he first met chaos. Adam's response to chaos transformed paradise into a wasteland. His silence introduced a whole new chaos to his descendants: violence and sexual perversion. The rest of Genesis details these stories of sex and violence: Abel's murder, Lot's incest with his daughters, and the rape of Dinah, to name a few.

Adam's struggle and failure have been repeated by every man. Our lives are full of chaos. Chaos is tragedy in a million disguises. It could be the fear of an uncertain future. It is a decision that needs to be made, when all possibilities look right. Chaos could be the loss of a job, a reduction in pay, the loss of a mate, a rebellious teenager, a bad medical prognosis. If we are honest, we know that chaos nags at us daily. Chaos is that darkness hovering over us every time we speak to our wives, work at our jobs, pay our bills, and try to make sense of our lives.

Adam taught us what not to do. Is there anything that teaches us the right response to the chaos of our lives?

Before one answers what it means to be a man, he must first decide upon his reference point. Where do men go to define themselves? Do they look to other men, their fathers, their churches? Do they look to movies, TV, psychology?

Most men are defined more by the culture around them than by the truth of God's Word. We must return to his revealed story if we are going to be the men God intended us to be. God has spoken to us in his Word and given us a wonderful design to follow. To understand that design, it will prove important and helpful to compare the Bible with pagan creation stories.

Let's take a quick look at how ancient culture typically defined men. What did the nations outside of Israel say about men? What did their gods look like? What were their men and women supposed to look like? How were they to act toward one another?

Though there are numerous creation accounts from all over the world, let's take a look at just two: one from ancient Babylon and one from ancient Greece. Just as we look to Genesis to understand ourselves, the Babylonians and Greeks looked to their myths to understand themselves. As you read these myths, keep in mind the Genesis creation story. The difference between the pagan myths and the Genesis story is startling.

THE BABYLONIAN STORY OF CREATION (THE BABYLONIANS CALLED IT *ENUMA ELISH*)

When the heavens and earth had no name, when there was no pasture land and there were no marshes, Apsu ("Sweet Water") and Tiamat ("Salt Water") were god and goddess. They were husband and wife, and they bore two children named Lahma and Lahamu. Then they bore Anshar and Kishar. There were many sons and grandsons.

Soon all the sons, the gods, gathered together and made much noise. They were becoming more and more powerful and boisterous. This bothered the peace and quiet of Apsu and Tiamat, their father and mother.

Apsu decided that he would murder his sons and grandsons so there would be silence once again. Tiamat was horrified. She was disgusted by them, but she wanted to act kindly toward them.

Apsu would not be dissuaded. He continued to plot the downfall of his progeny.

But one of his sons, Ea, heard of his devious plan. He cast a spell upon Apsu, his father, and then murdered him.

Then Ea and his wife, Damkina, had a son. His name was Marduk. He had four eyes and four ears. He was a splendid god, and his father rejoiced in the power and beauty of his son. He was the greatest of all the gods.

Another god, named Anu, made the four winds, and they disturbed Tiamat's waters. Because she was bothered by the winds, she in turn moved day and night, disturbing the other gods. They complained against Tiamat, their mother, and blamed her for Apsu's death.

Enraged, she created dragons and all sorts of awful beasts. She created demons, and they brought great chaos to the heavens.

Ea called his son, Marduk, to deal with Tiamat. Marduk, the great king, went out to battle Tiamat. He caused great winds to stir up the waters of Tiamat. She cast spells of magic. She spit poison. She opened her mouth to devour Marduk.

But Marduk cast an evil wind down her throat and then shot an arrow into her; it struck her heart and she died. He cast her body down and stood on it, boasting of his victory. He split her skull with his club. He cut her arteries and let the winds carry her blood to faraway places. Lastly he took her body and divided it into two parts: one part became the sky, and the other part became the earth.

Marduk finished creation. From the blood of a god, he created men to do the service of the gods, to attend to the needs of the gods.

The gods rejoiced in the majesty of Marduk and praised him greatly.

A GREEK STORY OF CREATION (THE GREEKS NAME THEIR CREATION STORY AFTER THE MALE GOD *KRONOS*)

In the beginning there was nothing. This nothing was called Chaos, the Void.

Soon Earth came into being so the gods would have something to stand on. Next came Tartarus, the underworld. Then Eros, love. He was very handsome and the strongest of the gods.

Chaos brought forth Night and Erebos. Night and Erebos brought forth Day and Space. Earth gave birth to Heaven and Sea.

The gods rested in Heaven but made their home on Mount Olympus.

Heaven and Earth gave birth to the Titans. The youngest of these was Kronos. He was an untamed son and he hated his father, Heaven.

Three more sons were born to Heaven and Earth. Each one was a fearsome, powerful monster that had fifty heads.

This was too much for Heaven, the father. He always hated his children, and so he imprisoned them in the dark regions of the earth.

Their mother, Earth, conspired against her husband. She offered to help her sons escape imprisonment. They were all terrified of their father except Kronos. His mother gave him a sickle she had made earlier.

Heaven came to Earth and tenderly spread himself over Earth. Kronos was waiting in secret. He struck his father with the sickle and killed him.

Before dying, Heaven cursed his children. He declared that they would all pay for their crime against him.

Kronos had his own children. It dawned on him one day that his children could do the same thing he did to his father. If he could kill his father, then they could kill him. When his wife, Rhea, gave birth to their children, he ate them whole.

Rhea prayed to Earth to hide her son, Zeus. She granted her request by hiding Zeus in the woods.

Rhea took a large stone and wrapped it up. She deceived Kronos to think that this was their son, Zeus. Believing this wrapped stone was his son, Kronos seized the bundle and gulped it down. He thought that this destroyed his son.

So Zeus became the greatest of the gods. Soon Zeus would destroy his father, Kronos.

"INFLAMED BY ANGER AND MADDENED BY LUST"

Both myths have common threads. The stories begin with chaos. In the Babylonian myth, heaven and earth had no name, and there was no farmable land. The Greek story is more obvious: in the beginning there was nothing, which was called Chaos.

In both stories, the male god is uncomfortable with the female god. She personifies chaos. She is mystery that must be violently murdered and dismembered. In the Babylonian story, Tiamat's divided body becomes the womb giving birth to earth and sky. In the Greek story, the female goddess, Earth, lures her husband sexually in order to destroy him.

The gods war against their own children. The gods and goddesses of the pagan myths murder fathers, brothers, wives, and children.

OF ADAM

They create humanity to work for them as slaves. They see humanity as evil and as having no dignity.

The stories end in chaos: death, destruction, sexual deviance. People are not nurtured; they are destroyed. *The pagan myths move from chaos to chaos.*

The pagan myths can only affirm what is already true about men. Men are violent and they are sexually perverse. The pagans shaped their gods in man's image. Man *as he was* became their point of reference. They could only speak of what was natural to men. They rarely, if ever, spoke of what man could become, of the dignity and beauty of manhood.

In the pagan myths, the men brought darkness to the land. Because the male gods were selfish, fearful, and ravenous, they brought chaos to their families. The pagan myths depicted a male god who lived for himself, a god who was the only purpose of his own existence.

Listen to what Cicero said about the Greek and Roman creation stories:

> The poets have represented the gods as inflamed by anger and maddened by lust, and have displayed to our gaze their wars and battles, their fights and wounds, their hatreds, enmities, and quarrels . . . their complaints and lamentations, the utter and unbridled license of their passions, their adulteries and imprisonments, their unions with human beings, and the birth of mortal progeny from an immortal parent.

In the ancient Near East, men feared chaos above everything. Men of old lived in perpetual terror of being thrown into chaos at any moment. They lived in fear of famine. They lived in fear of infertility. They lived in fear of marauding enemies. So what did they do with their chaos? They made gods in their image—gods of violence and sexual perversion. And they worshiped their gods with violence and sexual perversion to appease them, to persuade them to banish the chaos of their world. That is how many men *have* responded to chaos.

But how *can* men respond to the chaos of their lives? What is the biblical pattern?

CHAOS TO CREATION

In the Genesis story, man is made in the image of God. Christianity begins with God, not man. We are in his image. He is our reference point. And who is this God? Was he anything like the gods of the pagan myths?

Does God use violence and sexual perversion to confront his chaos? Not at all.

The Genesis creation story never affirms the violence and demanding sexual appetite of men. Instead the story gives a rich portrait of what man was in his perfect state and what man could be if he lived in the image of God. It is male and female, man and woman, living in harmony and mutual respect. The male is not terrified of the female. The female does not seek to destroy the male. They nurture each other, and together they tend the garden they live in.

Adam and Eve were to "till and keep the garden"; that is, they were called to protect and to nurture. Strength, the opposite of violence, is in the man to guard relationships, not to destroy them. Intimacy, the opposite of lust, is in the man to nurture people, not to use them for his selfish desires. Adam's first recorded words were relational and poetic: "She is bone of my bone and flesh of my flesh."

Throughout Genesis and the Old Testament, man is the mediator. He is the connection between the past and the future. He understands that he does not live for himself. He does not destroy his children. He does not forget his children. He knows that violence destroys children. He understands that sexual perversion corrupts children. He remembers the stories of old, the stories of his fathers and grandfathers. And he lives to transfer the story of God to the next generation, to his children and grandchildren. "When your children ask you in the future, 'These words and commandments and ordinances that God has commanded you—what do they mean?' Then you shall say to your children . . ." (Deuteronomy 6:20–21 author's translation).

There is one major similarity between Genesis and the pagan myths. It is recorded in Genesis 3, "The Fall of Man." Adam's disobedience did exactly what the pagan myths condoned. God moved from chaos to creation in Genesis 1 and 2. In Genesis 3, Adam moved from chaos to chaos in a world of beauty. Adam's disobedience set a dark world into motion—a world of sex and violence. The rest of Genesis portrays the results of the first man's sin: hatred, murder, racism, rape, incest, and adultery.

When a man moves into the mystery of life with rage and lust, he lives as the pagans live. He believes there is no hope in God. God is absent. God is silent. A man doesn't know what to do with the confusion of his life, so he rages and he lusts.

Rage makes men feel powerful. Violence causes us to take matters into our own hands and seek to correct an unjust God. Lust helps men forget. Fantasy is a selfish way of living for the present. It denies the pain of the past, and the hope of the future. With anger men are present, but they are dangerous. With lust men are absent, but they feel alive.

The book of Genesis tells a very different creation story. Yes, the story ends badly. But it begins beautifully. That is our hope. Beauty exists. There is meaning and order. Responding to the mystery of life with violence and sexual perversion pitches the world back into darkness. Genesis never condones this. Genesis invites us to return to our design, to become men of strength and intimacy, to honor our calling to become like God. The book of Revelation tells us we will make it one day. Everything in between these two books tells us how. It's the story of God. It must be remembered.

Chapter 6

A Call to Remember

Before he walked into the windowless building, he looked both ways, as if he were about to cross a dangerous intersection. His heart raced with both fear and excitement. He feared that he might be caught—or that he might not. He felt the excitement of being aroused and of being at risk. Even though this section of town was one his parishioners rarely visited, he wondered if someone he knew might just happen by on this day. But seeing no familiar face, he walked cautiously through the door marked "Adults Only."

During the next hour, he eagerly thumbed through magazines and stared at videos, looking up occasionally to reassure himself of his anonymity. In that time, he forgot all that was important to him: the rich evening of prayer he had enjoyed with good friends the night before; his wife, pregnant with their second child; his bright-eyed, two-year-old daughter; the growing church he pastored; the God whom he had known since his conversion in high school. He had to put all these out of his mind, because their presence would have spoiled his momentary indulgence.

After a while, he left as cautiously as he had entered, feeling both bored and aroused at the same time—and deeply unsatisfied. And during the long drive home, the initial fear and excitement of his "adventure" gave way to a familiar feeling of defeat.

Across town, another man was driving toward the same store. It was a frequently traveled road for him as well. But this time, during his agonizing journey, he noticed an old stone cathedral situated along the route. Suddenly he made a choice. He drove into the church parking lot. He stopped, got out, and walked toward the huge oak doors. Like the other man, he was fearful and excited, but he didn't need to look both ways before he entered. This man's fear was that his sudden choice—a better and different choice—would be short-lived. But maybe there was something noble within him, something prompting this choice, that was pressing for release.

He proceeded through the doors. Once inside, he walked quietly to the altar. There he lit a candle, knelt before it, and prayed. He was humbled and broken by the foolish choices he'd made in times past, and he was grateful that today something was different. He thought of his wife, his children, his colleagues in ministry, and he remembered God and worshiped him there.

After a time, he left the church, got in his car, and drove home. He was exhausted from the struggle. But he was hopeful for the first time in many years.

THE STRUGGLE IS REAL

You've just read two brief stories of two men. Their struggles are similar. Their choices weren't. In these stories, many men may recognize their own struggles with similar issues. Scores of men have fought shameful battles like these for years but have been too embarrassed to talk about them to anyone. They have felt alone. Other men who don't struggle with pornography may be unaware of more subtle addictions. They indulge in different passions: workaholism, materialism, overeating, the need for control, the need to be liked, an active fantasy life, masturbation. The list is endless, but the struggle is the same. All men fight against overwhelming desires and passions that defy restraint. And like the two men in the opening stories, some fight the battle well, while others know only defeat.

THE ROOT OF THE PROBLEM

If either of these men came to you for help, what would you say to him? What advice would you give him to deal with his problems?

Most advice-givers might go in one of several directions. "You need to be in fellowship with other believers," says one. "If you're in community with godly men and women, you'll be more likely to keep away from sinful patterns. Be accountable to someone."

"Read the Bible and memorize key passages," suggests another. "The man who keeps the word of God in his heart will not get entangled in the things of the world."

Yet another offers, "Flee temptation. Stay away from certain places that may cause you to stumble."

All of this advice is good, sound, and right. All of it has strong biblical backing. For some men, such exhortations have produced noticeable change. But for many others, the advice leaves them only more discouraged. Perhaps that's your reaction. Maybe you've been faithfully doing all of these things for years, and yet nothing has truly changed. You've had temporary successes, but your problem always comes back, and you feel more discouraged than ever.

I suggest we consider another approach to men's struggles—one that incorporates the good in the other advice given, but offers more. Instead of merely mustering up more energy to do something or to not do something, take a deeper look. Ask yourself: Why do we do what we do? Why do we choose to live in ways that are contrary to what we know to be true and right?

Men are created in God's image. By design, we are called to uniquely express something of him by how we live and relate in our world. We are designed to move, to speak, to create, to love. If our lives do not reflect this image, something is wrong. And what's wrong here is serious. A big choice is required of men, one that encompasses far more than the decision of whether to look at pornography. The wrong choice, when unrecognized, results in the violation of a man's essential nature.

Departure from our intended design is the root of the problem. And that departure is always a choice.

CREATED TO REMEMBER

We have already seen that a man lives out the image of God as he moves and speaks into the chaos of his world. Yet even more is involved in God's design for men. Genesis 1:27 tells us explicitly that God created man and woman "in his own image." In this passage, the word *man* is translated from the Hebrew word *zakar*, which means "the remembering one." What a curious word to describe a man. One might have expected a word meaning "the strong one," "the one who leads," or "the powerful one." But instead man is described as the one who remembers. Why?

What is a man supposed to remember? Should he be better at remembering where he left his keys? Should he work harder at recalling important dates, like anniversaries and birthdays? If that's what it means for a man to be the remembering one, then all but the most compulsive among us are in trouble. The idea of remembering carries a far more profound significance. It means first that we have something important to remember; second, it suggests we have a reason to remember.

SOMETHING TO REMEMBER

All of us have several longtime friends who have shared in important parts of our lives. For me those friends were my colleagues in a campus ministry. It has been several years now since we've had a reunion. But whenever this group of cherished friends gets together, each of us knows what will happen. We'll enjoy a good meal, catch up on one another's lives; and finally, sometime during the evening, storytelling will begin. This part is not something we discuss beforehand, nor is it something for which any of us prepares. It simply happens.

Someone begins to recount a particular event from our shared past, and everyone listens intently. It is a story every man in the group has heard innumerable times, but that doesn't diminish interest in the tale. In fact, so familiar are we with every story that the teller is often corrected by someone who remembers an important part of the plot. Anticipation builds as the story gains momentum and moves toward its hilarious climax. When that moment is reached, we all burst into uproarious laughter, with tears streaming down our cheeks as we try to catch our breath. And when we regain our composure, a request is made: "Roger, tell us the one about. . ." And the cycle continues into the night.

Why do we tell these stories? Is it because we're desperate for fun? (Some have suggested this.) Is it because we're living in the past and unable to move ahead? (Some have suggested this too.) There is a far more important reason.

The stories we tell are not the point. In themselves, they are nothing more than entertaining vignettes of shared lives. They are fun and sometimes silly, but somehow they matter. Their value lies in their power to point us toward something. They remind us of another day, another time, years ago when we worked together in a student ministry. It was a time when we saw God work in our lives and in the lives of the students in our charge. Significant things happened, sorrowful things happened, miraculous things happened. God did a work in our midst, and we tell our stories to remind us of those days.

It's only fitting that our group of men tells stories to one another. After all, men have been built that way. We are the "remembering ones," created to recall the past, created to tell stories.

Remembering is a theme repeated throughout the Bible. When the people of God gathered for worship, they confessed their sins and prayed, and one of their leaders stood among them and began to recount the works of God:

> You saw the suffering of our forefathers in Egypt; you heard their cry at the Red Sea. You sent miraculous signs and wonders against Pharaoh, against all his officials and all the people of his land, for you knew how arrogantly the Egyptians treated them. You made a name for yourself, which remains to this day. You divided the sea before them, so that they passed through it on dry ground, but you hurled their pursuers into the depths, like a stone into mighty waters. By day you led them with a pillar of cloud, and by night with a pillar of fire to give them light on the way they were to take. (Nehemiah 9:9–12)

History was told and retold in remembered stories. Think of the number of times in the Bible when the works of God are recounted. Why so many? In the Old Testament, God was eager to reveal himself to a people who lived in the midst of chaos. The elders knew that stories of God's loyal love were a necessary anchor for continued trust. Their retelling of old stories conveyed a vital message: "God is faithful to his people. Time and time again he has intervened on our behalf. He has proved his goodness. And he is the same God now as he was then. So take courage. Have faith. Don't forget what he is like and what he has done."

Habakkuk, the prophet who rages against God for his apparent inactivity and accuses him of being deaf and blind, finds hope as he remembers, and prays: "LORD, I have heard of your fame; I stand in awe of your deeds, O LORD. Renew them in our day, in our time make them known; in wrath remember mercy" (Habakkuk 3:2). Habakkuk was remembering the revealed history of God.

Once, as the Philistines approached Israel to do battle, the prophet Samuel offered a sacrifice. The Lord thundered and threw the enemy into a panic, enabling Israel to rout them easily. Samuel then took a stone and set it up, naming it Ebenezer, which means "Thus far the Lord helped us." From that day on, whenever the people passed by that stone, they remembered the faithfulness of God.

We are the remembering ones. We are created to remember the words of God and the works of God. Men are called to remember God by faithfully telling others who he is and what he has done. But why? What is the purpose of remembering?

A REASON TO REMEMBER

> Only be careful, and watch yourselves closely so that you do not forget the things your eyes have seen or let them slip from your heart as long as you live. Teach them to your children and to their children after them. Remember the day you stood before the LORD your God at Horeb, when he said to me, "Assemble the people before me to hear my words so that they may learn to revere me as long as they live in the land and may teach them to their children." (Deuteronomy 4:9–10)

Several years ago I went through a particularly difficult time. For months everything in my life felt like a battle. Clients in my counseling ministry presented unusually severe and seemingly insurmountable problems. Friends of mine were undergoing extremely hard times. The horrors of living in this fallen world seemed very close.

I began to feel a little crazy. At any given moment, I felt the overwhelming urge to either cry or fight. A rather innocuous song would come on the radio, and I would begin to weep. A driver would edge over into my lane, and I had to resist the compulsion to run him or her off the road. A child sitting in his mother's grocery cart would smile at me, and my eyes would fill with tears. Yet if the checkout line didn't move fast enough, I'd angrily look for a manager to correct the problem quickly. Sadness and fury. Back and forth.

Finally I went to a good friend and colleague and told him what was going on. He listened intently before giving me this solemn reply: "It's a difficult thing to have entered into the battle and to realize there's no way out."

I was stunned by his answer—yet I knew it was true. Over the course of several years, I had begun to make some choices to fight a greater battle. I had chosen to open my eyes more and more to the terrible realities of a fallen world. In my twenties, I had lived as a man who was content to let others fight the big fights, while I stood on the sidelines and offered food and water. But that stance was changing, and I knew it. Facing the future felt terrifying now. The reality of it brought tears and anger: tears because I wanted to go home (wherever home was); and anger because of what I feared was ahead, and because of what might be required of me.

After talking with my friend, I remembered a few of the stories my father had told me about World War II, in which he had fought as a young man. I called my father one night and asked him if he would write down for me some of his reflections about being in the war.

The next week, my dad's letter arrived. He eloquently described the days leading up to the invasion of Omaha Beach. The feelings of the men. The words of their commanders. Landing on the beaches. Crawling over the bodies of fallen comrades. Fatigue. Hardship. The cause that gave him courage, and the fear that urged him to retreat. And interspersed throughout the description of battle, my father's words spoke of prayer, of fear, of knowing God in the midst of terrible and difficult times.

I devoured the letter. It let me know a part of my father that I hadn't previously known. But more importantly, it gave me hope. Something of him, something of what he remembered, had been passed on to me. And I know now in a deeper way something of the ways of God.

My friend's words and my father's letter suggest the reason why we are to remember. Men are called to pass on something important to future generations: not just a passing on of history but a passing on of the memory of God in our lives. It is the act of placing our present lives into a larger perspective. Indeed, the psalmist testifies to the hope and courage that Israel's stories gave him:

> We have heard with our ears, O God; our fathers have told us what you did in their days, in days long ago. With your hand you drove out the nations and planted our fathers; you crushed the peoples and made our fathers flourish. It was not by their sword that they won the land, nor did their arm bring them victory; it was your right hand, your arm, and the light of your face, for you loved them. (Psalm 44:1–3)

My father didn't give me answers to my struggle. But his remembering gave me courage to go on in the midst of it. His stories gave me hope.

THE REFUSAL TO REMEMBER

Most men are known for their silence. Their children rarely learn about their father's past—his experiences, his failures, his struggles with faith. Instead of passing something on to his children, he remains silent. He acts as if he has no memory. Why?

Think back to the two men I described at the beginning of this chapter. How does the idea of man as the "remembering one" relate to a struggle with sexual sin—or with any other sin?

Think about it. The man who entered the adult bookstore had to put out of his mind all that was dear to him. He couldn't "enjoy" those sinful pleasures while any thoughts of his wife or children or ministry were still in his mind. For those moments, however brief, he had to put out of his mind God as well, to honor his sinful choices.

Consider a time when you willfully moved—physically or mentally— toward something you knew was wrong. At that moment, what was your relationship with God like? Was it close? Were you enjoying intimacy with him? Of course not. If he had been in the picture, you couldn't have continued in your sinful direction. Such is the nature of idolatry—the seeking of something other than God to satisfy one's desires. Sinful choices require that God be forgotten. In this sense, forgetting is about more than just misplacing car keys. It is an active and willful choice—a refusal to remember.

The apostle Paul paints a vivid picture of what happened when men "exchanged the glory of the immortal God for images [idols] made to look like mortal man" (Romans 1:23). "God gave them over in the sinful desires of their hearts to sexual impurity" (Romans 1:24). Verse 28 is especially worthy of our attention: "Furthermore, since they did not think it worthwhile to retain the knowledge of God, he gave them over to a depraved mind, to do what ought not to be done." These people forgot God. The result was serious sin.

Although men knew the truth about God, they came to a place where they saw no value in keeping that truth foremost in their minds. They fashioned predictable gods, ones that would not interfere with their sinful choices. What is a man doing when he goes into a bookstore or when he fantasizes? What is happening when he must be in control, and he requires others to line up with his way of thinking? What is a man's motive when his greatest passion is to be liked? In each of these situations, the root problem is the failure to believe that God is enough. "This life I'm living is not working. God is not treating me the way I deserve. Life just doesn't feel good. I want something or someone that either makes me feel good or places me in control. Trusting God is not producing the results I want. Therefore I must put him aside. I must choose to forget God for a time and to replace him with something more pleasurable."

We men come by this quite naturally. Adam, before the Fall, had something to remember. He knew much about the character of God from witnessing God's creative work and from his conversations with God. Adam knew what God had given him to do, what God had provided for him, and what his own limits were. Yet we've already seen that Adam did not act on what he knew to be true. When the serpent tempted Eve, Adam didn't speak. His memory failed him. More accurately, he refused to remember.

Am I suggesting that men should establish "story time" each night for their families? That every time he is tempted, a man should recite Bible passages that recount the works of God? Will these things really help? Perhaps. But they may only put more pressure on a man to do things right. Something more is called for: a change of heart. Unless men honestly face their stubborn delight in forgetting and their commitment to passions stronger than their desire for God, lasting change will never occur.

THE CALL TO REMEMBER

As a young Christian, I thought it incredible that a group of people who had witnessed the Red Sea parting could forget what God had done and return to the worship of false gods. Soon after their miraculous deliverance from the hands of the Egyptians, the Israelites were again committing sin. And the Bible reports scores of incidents throughout Israel's history when people knew the goodness of God but still pursued other paths to life.

These stories used to surprise me. But today, when I face the realities in my own life, I'm not surprised at all. I am a believing man, a man who has seen God's hand obviously working in my life. And yet at times, I still search for something other than God to give me satisfaction and fulfillment. And in so doing, I fail to remember what is true.

After three years, Jesus' time with his disciples was coming to an end. One evening, Jesus called them together for the Passover meal. This group of men had been with him, had seen his miracles with their own eyes, and would soon witness his death and resurrection. To these men Jesus said, "Do this in remembrance of me." Surely, of all people, they would not need a symbol to help them remember Christ. After everything they had witnessed and heard, how could they possibly forget?

Yet Jesus knew these men as he knows us. And he knew of their inclination to forget. Consider their petty discussion, recorded in Luke 22:24, which occurred only moments after Jesus had foretold his death: "Also a dispute arose among them as to which of them was considered to be greatest." Even before Jesus had left their presence, they had forgotten his words. Already they were departing from the life to which he had called them.

OF ADAM

The two men described in the beginning of this chapter were both faced with the choice to remember. Both men struggled. And both men worshiped. The first refused to remember, and ultimately worshiped at the altar of a false god. The second, hearing Christ's call to remember him, worshiped the true God.

Chapter 7

He Was There and He Was Silent

"I believe in God even when he is silent."

It was the longest day of his week. He was a professor at a small university, and he had to work two jobs to make ends meet. He awoke early on this Wednesday morning to counsel an out-of-town client over the phone. Afterward he rushed to meet a student for breakfast. Then he hurried to the office for his weekly faculty meeting. As soon as that meeting ended, he taught a three-hour class. Then lunch with another student, followed by four consecutive hours of counseling. To finish the day, he spent an hour with a colleague, discussing plans for an upcoming seminar.

As he drove home that night, he was drained and exhausted. He had talked with friends, students, former students, colleagues, and clients from 5:30 in the morning until 6:30 at night. Once again he had given of himself to the point of exhaustion. While still on the road home he decided he had nothing left to give. More than anything else, he wanted to be alone. He thought briefly about how he might be able to get away for a few days.

Listening to the radio, he dreamed of his imaginary cabin tucked away in the Montana mountains. No hassles. No requests. No criticisms. But he was torn by another thought, one that gnawed at him, even though it was pleasant. As tired as he was, he couldn't wait to be with the people he loved the most: his wife and son.

As he pulled into the driveway, he sensed a rage rising within him. His body tensed, and he felt a familiar wall rise up. He knew exactly what would happen when he entered the house. He rehearsed it in his mind as he pulled into the garage: his son would want to play, and his wife would want to know everything about his day. And she would want to tell him everything about her day. She would list everything she had faced since he had left that morning. She'd ask him to look at the dryer or fix the toilet or unclog the garbage disposal.

As he sat in the car he felt the weight of what his family would ask of him. He began to blame his wife for his anger and frustration. *She asks too much. She doesn't understand the frustrations of my work. She doesn't appreciate the sacrifices I make for her. She never gives me a break,* he complained to himself.

When he walked into the den, his wife greeted him with a question that millions of wives ask their husbands every day. It was a simple question requiring only a simple answer. Why did it make him angry? She wasn't asking for something he could not give, like an answer to a complex math problem. She was asking for something he *could* give—but he guarded it the way a wild-eyed pirate protects his most secret treasure.

She asked the question, "How was your day?"

He had spent his long day talking—counseling, chatting, teaching, discussing future plans. And now, after thirteen hours of talking, he came up with his usual answer to her question. He looked straight into her eyes and said one word: "Fine."

He hoped that would end the conversation. Immediately he picked up the mail and pretended it was more pressing than her question. Yet he was well aware that she was asking for more than how his day had gone. She wanted him to share his life with her, to enter into conversation, to touch her loneliness with his words and presence. But he refused to give.

Like so many nights before, he turned silent with the one he loved. He could speak with students and clients, but he hid from his wife. Later that night, in the privacy of his mind, he agonized over his stubborn, silent retreat. He asked himself the usual questions: *Why do I despise her questions? I love my wife, but I use exhaustion as an excuse to dismiss her. Why was I silent? Today was a particularly long day. But even on easier days, I run from the ones I love. Why?*

WHAT IS WRONG WITH MEN?

I understand this man. I understand him because, almost daily, I go through this very routine and ask the same questions. Yet my work both in the Scriptures and in the counseling office has convinced me that every man struggles with a deep and chosen silence. The first time I taught about the silence of men, I was mobbed by wives who exclaimed, "My husband is silent, too! What can I do to get him to talk with me?" And a few men surreptitiously approached me and whispered, "I thought I was the only one. You struggle with this, too?"

Every man wrestles with the tension between a design he cannot escape and his daily violation of that design. The design of every man is to talk and be talked to. Men want to love and be loved, but they feel blocked inside. Something will not let their emotions and feelings out.

Can we be helped? Can we change? Of course, but a godly man's journey begins in a strange way. His journey begins with facing failure, not achieving success. It begins with an honest evaluation of what is wrong.

The solution to a problem always begins with the right assessment of the problem. We need a clear understanding of what is wrong with us before we can change and live according to our design. The Scriptures provide that understanding. They speak of a man—the first man—who had the problem of silence. Let's take a careful look at this familiar story to see what the problem is and where it began.

ADAM WAS THERE...

And the serpent was more cunning than all the wild animals that the Lord God had made. And the serpent said to the woman, "Did God really say, 'You shall not eat from all the trees of the garden'?" And the woman said to the serpent, "We may eat from the fruit of the trees of the garden. [But] from the fruit of the tree in the middle of the garden God did say that you may not eat from it, and you may not touch it, lest you die." And the serpent said to the woman, "Certainly, you will not die. For God knows that on the day you eat from it your eyes will be opened and you will be like God knowing good and evil." And the woman saw that the tree was good for food, and that it was pleasant to the eyes, and that it was desirable for wisdom, and she took from its fruit and she ate. And she gave also to her husband, who was with her, and he ate. And the eyes of them both were opened, and they knew that they were naked, and they sewed fig leaves together and made coverings for themselves. (Genesis 3:1–7 author's translation)

Throughout its history, the church commonly has blamed Eve for the downfall of the human race. Most people assume that while the serpent and Eve conversed Adam was elsewhere. They suppose that after Eve sinned, she found Adam and tempted him to eat of the forbidden fruit. And often Eve is denounced because she attempted to battle wits with the serpent but, in her weakness, succumbed to his craftiness. They have been taught that Eve made the first step in sinning against God, and that Adam merely followed her example. Some interpreters have even suggested that Adam ate of the fruit so Eve would not live alone in her sin.

Indeed, Adam is made to look noble in light of the petulance of his "weaker vessel." But what if Adam was there with Eve for the entire conversation? What if he was standing beside her and heard for himself the serpent's spin on the truth? What if his disobedience began not in the eating of the fruit but in his refusal to talk with the serpent or his wife?

If Adam was there but silent, it sheds new light on the problem with men. The church's interpretation of Genesis has perhaps allowed men to blame women for their problems—just as Adam blamed Eve—and to not face up to their failures. But it becomes a different situation altogether if Adam was standing next to Eve while the serpent tempted her. Then his silence becomes a sin, with far reaching implications.

There are four reasons why we believe Adam was present at the temptation: (1) his silence fits the immediate context in Genesis 1–3; (2) Genesis 3:6 says he was there; (3) the style of the entire account recorded in Genesis 3:1–7 suggests Eve turned immediately to Adam and gave him the fruit; and (4) other men in Genesis lived out this age-old problem of Adam's silence, suggesting that his silence became a pattern in his male descendants.

ADAM, THE IMAGE-BEARER, DEFIES HIS IMAGE

First, let's look at the immediate context of this passage. We'll do this by comparing Genesis 3 with Genesis 1. In Genesis 1 God confronts darkness and chaos: "The earth was formless and void." We have previously seen that God created the world in a unique way. He spoke into the darkness and brought forth order, beauty, and relationship. The Jewish community has a unique expression to describe this Creator: "He who spoke and the world came into being." He is a God who uses language to establish relationship. He does not retreat from darkness and chaos. Rather, he speaks into it. And after his creative activity, he keeps the Sabbath.

In Genesis 3 Adam—the man who was to represent God—acts very differently than his God. As in Genesis 1, the story in Genesis 3 begins with chaos. "And the serpent was more cunning than all the wild animals that the Lord God had made." He spoke to the woman, "Did God really say . . .?" We observed in chapter 5 that a serpent represented chaos. People in the ancient Near East believed that a serpent symbolized deceit and confusion. In Genesis 3:1 chaos reappears in the form of a serpent who uses deceit to confuse Adam and Eve.

But what happens in the face of chaos? Ironically, it is Eve who reflects the image of God more clearly than Adam, because she speaks with the serpent. But what about Adam? If Adam was there, he was not speaking. Chaos had entered his perfect world, and he stood dumbfounded in its confusion and darkness. The Scriptures record no instruction from God to Adam about what to say to the serpent. So Adam said nothing.

Adam, then, was a silent man, a passive man. Like many men in history, he was physically present but emotionally absent. He fades into the background of the story, rather than standing front and center on the stage. In contrast, God appeared front and center on the scene in Genesis 1 and spoke to transform a wasteland into a paradise. Adam, on the other hand, disappeared. His sin began with his silence. He was designed to speak but he said nothing. He listened to the serpent, he listened to his wife, he accepted the fruit, and *then* he ate.

Adam was passive three times before he ate the forbidden fruit.

God's speaking brought creation out of chaos; Adam's silence brought chaos back to creation. Remember that God used language to establish relationship; Adam used silence to destroy relationship. God rested after his creative work; Adam labored harder as a result of his silence. Adam ruined paradise by failing to do something. Adam, the image-bearer, did not reflect his God, because he chose to be absent, silent, and forgetful of God's command.

ADAM, *WHO WAS WITH HER*

There is a second basis for believing that Adam was present during the temptation. The text explicitly states that Adam was there. "And the woman saw that the tree was good for food, and that it was pleasant to the eyes, and that it was desirable for wisdom, and she took from its fruit and she ate. And she gave also to her husband, *who was with her*, and he ate" (Genesis 3:6, author's translation and emphasis). This simple but indicting phrase has been largely ignored. But it shouldn't be. It's an important phrase. And the Hebrew is even more straightforward. '*Imha* is composed of two Hebrew words that are translated "with her." The Hebrew construction is a combination of the preposition *'im*, meaning "with," and the feminine third-person personal pronoun *ha*, meaning "her."

When *'im* is used in the Hebrew Bible, it denotes close proximity, even to the point of sexual intercourse. Other prepositions could have been chosen to show association in this verse, but the use of *'im* indicates not only close association but physical proximity. A good translation of this phrase would be "right there with her."

Many verses confirm this interpretation of the phrase "who was with her." Consider just one, Judges 13:9. This verse appears in the story of Samson, which is told in Judges 13–16. Before Samson was born, the angel of the Lord appeared to Samson's mother. Now, typically the angel of the Lord appeared to men. Why, then, did he appear to Samson's mother and not to his father, Manoah?

Samson's mother was barren, and the angel of the Lord appeared to promise her a son. He told her she must consecrate her son as a Nazirite, a man who must never cut his hair. The woman rushed to tell her husband of the angel's appearance and announcement, but Manoah was skeptical. He asked the Lord to reappear and tell *him* what to do with the boy. Perhaps he did not trust the word of his wife, or maybe he was slow to grasp what God had already said.

In any case, the Lord answered Manoah's prayer, but not exactly in the way he had asked. Listen to the report: "God listened to Manoah, and the angel of God came again to the woman as she sat in the field; but her husband Manoah *was not with her*" (Judges 13:9 author's translation and emphasis). Here we see the same phrase—*'imha*—again, only this time it is used with the negative *lo*.

In Judges 13 the angel of the Lord appears to the woman, but her husband, Manoah, is literally *lo 'imha—not with her*. He is physically not there. In Genesis 3 the serpent appears and speaks with another woman, and *her* husband, Adam, is *'imha*—right there with her. So we see this Hebrew word used in two instances. In both cases, the meaning clearly involves physical proximity: Manoah was *not there* with his wife, and Adam *was there*. With these clearly stated passages from Scripture, the burden of proof rests upon the traditional interpretation to prove that Adam was *not* with Eve. The text indicates he was.

EVE TURNED TO HER HUSBAND

The third reason we believe Adam was there is that Genesis 3:1–7 is presented as one narrative time unit. Nothing in this passage suggests a time lapse between Eve's eating the fruit and her offering it to Adam. And there is nothing in verse 6 to suggest that Adam was away during the temptation. Nor is there any evidence that Eve ate of the fruit by herself and afterward went to find Adam. If we read the narrative as it is presented, we never see any time break in verse 6. Instead we see Eve take the fruit, eat the fruit, and then immediately give it to her silent, passive husband, who *was with her*.

Once again the burden of proof rests upon traditional interpretation to prove that there was a time break between Eve eating the fruit and then departing the scene to find Adam.

ADAM AGAIN AND AGAIN

The author of Genesis is a storyteller. He has revealed the plot and the problem in the first three chapters. The next forty-seven chapters play out the same theme in countless fascinating stories. As with any good story, Genesis repeats the same themes and events. And the theme of masculine silence appears again and again.

Several of the men portrayed in Genesis choose to be silent and oblivious, absent and forgetful. And they consistently get into trouble whenever they choose silence over involvement, or forgetting over remembering. For example: Abram (later called Abraham), rather than trusting God's timetable, heeded Sarai's suggestion and slept with his servant Hagar. "And Sarai said to Abram, 'Look, the Lord has prevented me from bearing children: Please go in to my handmaid so I might obtain children by her.' *And Abram listened to the voice of Sarai*. And Sarai Abram's wife took Hagar her maid the Egyptian, *and gave her to her husband Abram* to be his wife" (Genesis 16:2–3, author's translation and emphasis).

Note the similarities between Adam and Abraham. Like Adam, Abraham was passive in his interaction with his wife. Although Sarah was wrong, Abraham listened to her. Recall that God punished Adam for listening to his wife. And just as Eve gave forbidden fruit to her husband, so Sarah gave her handmaid to Abraham—and he took her! Abraham was silent and passive. And his silence still speaks, four thousand years later.

Ishmael, Hagar's son—whose descendants comprise the Arab nations—despises Israel to this day.

Consider another example. Lot chose to remain oblivious to the blatant sin of Sodom, a city that was the epitome of evil. Lot actually offered his daughters to a group of perverted rapists. His action is not unlike that of Abraham and Isaac, both of whom jeopardized their wives by offering them to foreign kings. They are examples to us of what many men are like today. They are weak men, who sacrifice the women in their lives out of cowardice. Like Adam, such men force their wives to step into the chaos for them. Like Noah, they harm their children for years—even generations—with their drunkenness. In his drunken stupor, Lot did not know he was having sexual relations with his own daughters. His drunkenness led to incest, which produced sons who later warred continually with Israel.

Perhaps the most enlightening story is told in Genesis 38. It is an obscure and often ignored story. But it deserves careful notice, because it powerfully reenacts the story of the first sin.

Judah went to Canaan to find a wife. He married a woman named Shua, and she bore Judah three sons. "Shua conceived and bore a son, and she named him Er. Again she conceived and bore a son whom she named Onan. Yet again she bore a son, and she named him Shelah" (Genesis 38:3–5 author's translation).

Judah clearly had no trouble carrying out the divine command to multiply and fill the earth. But like every other story in Genesis, chaos entered the scene. Judah's firstborn son was wicked in God's eyes, and God struck him down. The second son, Onan, was commanded to practice a form of leviratic marriage to care for his dead brother's wife, Tamar, and carry on the family name. But Onan knew the children would not be his own, and neither would the inheritance. So rather than doing what God required, Onan spilled his semen on the ground. In doing so, he refused to perpetuate the memory of his brother (and his father, Judah, as well). In essence, he refused to remember. And what was God's response to this memory lapse? He took Onan's life, also.

Now, put yourself in Judah's shoes. You, like your fathers before you, desperately want a son to carry on your memory and name. And you realize that God's promise to Abraham is, as always, just one generation away from obliteration. In short, no children means no promise. (That is why children were so important to the first Hebrew families. If they did not have children, then God's promise would be broken.) You've fathered three sons, but you've lost your firstborn, the one in whom you'd placed your highest hope. And now you give your second son to his brother's wife so that she will bear children. And he dies, too. The question for you is this: Will you give your third son as well—your last hope? Will you trust God with this chaos?

Judah did not. And the author of Genesis tells the truth about him: "Then Judah said to his daughter-in-law Tamar, 'Remain a widow in your father's house until my son Shelah grows up'—*for he feared that he too would die*, like his brothers" (Genesis 38:11 author's translation and emphasis). Judah feared. He was the chosen one. His third son was his last hope. Had he trusted God, Judah would have given his third son. But instead he froze in the face of chaos. He patronized Tamar and merely brushed the problem away.

TRAGEDY AWAITS THOSE WHO ARE SILENT

What happens when men forget God and are silent? What is the result when they refuse to move sacrificially in response to God's promise? Tragically, they invite others to step into the chaos of their world.

Chaos for Judah was the unpredictable future. What would happen to his third son if he gave him to Tamar? The uncertainty of the future paralyzed Judah. Perhaps he thought that sending Tamar away would make the problem disappear.

But the problem came back. His weakness and deceit found him out. Listen to the rest of the story:

Judah's wife died. After his time of mourning was accomplished, he went to another city to shear his sheep. "When Tamar was told, 'Your father-in-law is going up to Timnah to shear his sheep,' she put off her widow's garments, put on a veil, wrapped herself up, and sat down at the entrance to Enaim. She saw that Shelah was grown up, yet she had not been given to him in marriage" (Genesis 38:13–14). Judah had not followed through on his promise to provide his last son as Tamar's husband. But Tamar, not being the passive woman that too many in the church today value, set out to rectify the problem. She showed more concern to continue the line of Abraham than Judah did.

Judah saw Tamar "and thought her to be a prostitute." Another man in Genesis oblivious to the reality around him. He slept with Tamar without knowing who she was, and then went on his way. Three months later Judah heard that Tamar was pregnant. As a man of justice, he flew into a rage and commanded that his daughter-in-law be burned, since she had not remained faithful.

But Tamar, unlike her mother Eve, did something cunning in response to this man's weakness. Because Judah had mistaken Tamar for a prostitute, he had asked her for sexual favors. Tamar had agreed but had required that Judah hand over his ring, cord, and staff. One scholar has remarked that these things were the modern equivalent of Judah's driver's license and credit cards. In a brilliant move, Tamar laid a trap for her father-in-law. The daughter of Eve reversed Eve's disobedience. Eve failed to use her cunning to defeat the serpent. Tamar used her brilliance to fulfill the cultural mandate. Tamar played the part until the perfect moment. As a powerless woman, she had to convict an oblivious but powerful man. According to Judah's command, she was taken out to be burned. On the way, she said to her executors, "Oh, by the way, the man who owns this ring, cord, and staff—he is the father of my child." Judah was trapped. He had to admit the truth. After years of lying to Tamar, he responded honestly, "This woman is more righteous than I." How did God respond? He responded by blessing Tamar with twin sons.

Judah's silence, oblivion, and deceit required Tamar to step into the uncertainty of his world. His silence was a denial of God, because he did not trust God for the future. It was Judah's stubborn paralysis that threatened his seed. He thought that protecting his interests would save his last son. But he was wrong. Had it not been for Tamar, the promise of God would have died with Judah's last son. Had it not been for Tamar, there would have been no David. Had it not been for Tamar, there would have been no Christ. In this story, Judah had a myopic, selfish vision. It was Tamar who invited Judah to a larger, selfless vision.

Like Adam, Abraham, and Lot, Judah did not comprehend the far-reaching consequences of his actions. His silence impacted generations of humanity. The New Testament memorializes Tamar's bravery and cunning by including her in Matthew's genealogy of Christ: "An account of the genealogy of Jesus the Messiah, the son of David, the son of Abraham. Abraham was the father of Isaac, and Isaac the father of Jacob, and Jacob the father of Judah and his brothers, and Judah the father of Perez and Zerah by Tamar" (Matthew 1:1–3 author's translation).

Adam was not alone in his silence. He was a man not unlike us. Chaos entered his world and he chose to forget. He was passive. He chose silence and was absent. His choice to be silent set the pattern for men's disobedience since that time.

ADAM WAS SILENT . . .

Adam was not only silent with the serpent, he was also silent with Eve. He never reminded her of God's word. He never called her to a larger vision. He did not join his wife in battling wits with the serpent. He passively listened to her speak, rather than speaking with her in mutual respect.

I am not saying that Adam should have spoken *for* Eve—or *to* her, as a father speaks to a child or as a superior speaks to an inferior. Many men make that mistake. Nor am I suggesting that men are to speak and women are to keep silent. Both men and women are created in God's image to speak. This is just where the first man sinned.

Adam disobeyed by failing to speak with the serpent and with his wife. He was absent and passive. His silence was symbolic of his refusal to be involved with Eve. And God punished Adam for his silence. "To Adam he said, 'Because you listened to your wife and ate from the tree about which I commanded you, "You must not eat of it," Cursed is the ground because of you; through painful toil you will eat of it all the days of your life'" (Genesis 3:17). God punished Adam for eating the forbidden fruit. But he also punished him for listening to his wife. Adam's disobedience was a process. Adam was silent and then he ate from the tree. His disobedience did not begin with his eating but with his silence. Disobeying God was a result of retreating from his wife. It was a silent man who eventually broke God's clear command.

SILENCE IS DEADLY

Like every man, I am silent just like Adam was silent. Sometimes I stand dumbfounded in the face of my confusion. When my wife asks me to share even the smallest part of myself, I occasionally bristle. When she cries, I may become angry with her. Her tears frighten me, because I don't know what to do with them. When she tells me I have done something wrong, I defend myself to the bitter end. If she finds fault with me, I find ten things wrong with her. I refuse to be wrong. I use words, I speak; but I use words to destroy relationship—as the serpent did in the garden.

Yet if my wife were able to scratch beneath the surface of my anger, she would find that I am ashamed of what is inside of me. What if I share my most intimate thoughts, dreams, and doubts—and she rejects me? Recall my story. I am a man who feels like an impostor. I already assume that I have nothing to offer. It is better, I wrongly think, to hide behind my silence.

But silence is not golden—it is deadly. Adam's silence was lethal. It brought the severing of relationship. And ultimately it brought death.

What does my silence do to my wife? It points a finger at her and blames her for wanting too much. Like Adam, I want to blame my wife for all the chaos of my world. "[Adam] said, 'The woman you put here with me—she gave me some fruit from the tree, and I ate it'" (Genesis 3:12). Blaming her takes the responsibility off me. My silence asks my wife to step into the confusion of my life. It requires her to pursue me in every interaction. How many times have I asked her, in sheer frustration, this question: "What do you want me to do? If you would give me an exact list, then I could meet your needs and you would be happy!" Give me a list. Then I'll never fail. I will know what to do every time. Being a man who feels inadequate and incompetent, it is important that I am never wrong, that I am not blamed.

And so men disappear into their work, their hobbies, and their sports. Things that matter less than relationship. Silence or disappearing becomes our best defense against fear.

That is exactly where the problem lies. My silence is a defense *against* chaos, not an entry *into* chaos. When we refuse to enter the chaos of our lives, we miss a grand opportunity. God created men in his image to create, to make a difference, to leave a legacy. He created men to bring redemption to a tragic world. He created them strong to protect the boundaries of those around him. He created them to have vision for other people.

But every man has felt the touch of tragedy. He has been damaged by his father, mother, grandparents, wife, children, superiors, business partners. Every man knows all too well that this world is dangerous. He knows the risk of sticking his neck out, whether it be relationship or work. Many men are convinced that the confusion of relationships and the uncertainty of the future can destroy them. So they remain silent. When men are silent, though, they deny the existence and goodness of God. That thought troubles me. I count myself as one who believes in God. But when I am silent, I live as an atheist: I give witness to my belief that chaos is more powerful than God.

Speaking is the gateway to relationship. Silence is the gatekeeper. The Hebrew Bible teaches us that words usher us out of silence and connect us to God. And being powerfully present in our words is a potent opportunity to bring life into areas where death reigns. But along with that opportunity comes a terrifying warning. Our silence destroys. There is no middle ground. Rabbi Pinchas of Koritz summarizes it well: "The world is like a book that can be read in either direction. There is the power of creation, to make something from nothing. And there is the power of destruction, to make nothing out of something."

Every moment of my life, I stand in the balance between creation and destruction. Silence destroys. Speaking creates. Even though I am a silent man, I want to be a man who speaks, who is present, who—like his God—makes something from nothing.

Conclusion to Part I

A man can be understood by knowing the questions that burn hotly within him. For many men, one question stands out among others as the one that matters most: "What should I do?" When men feel their deepest agony, that is the question they ask.

When a man finds himself in a place where that question cannot be answered, he moves to a place where it can. When he looks around and realizes he has wandered into a confusing situation where courage and creativity are required, he finds a way to return to the sphere of management, to some activity or responsibility where his skill and know-how are useful, where his inadequacy and fear will not be exposed, where the courage to live in an unpredictable world is not required; in short, he retreats to where he can find an answer to his burning question.

When a man flees the terror of mystery for the comforts of management, he compromises himself. A man ruled by the demand that he always know what to do cannot experience the deep joys of manhood. He has violated his calling and betrayed his nature.

God calls a man to speak into darkness, to remember who God is and what he has revealed about life, and—with that memory uppermost in his mind—to move into his relationships and responsibilities with the imaginative strength of Christ.

God is telling a story, a story full of life, love, and grace, a story of hating evil and honoring good, a story rich in drama, poetry, and passion. As we see his story told through our lives, we find the courage to handle the inevitable confusion of life. We find the strength to move ahead, to take risks, to relate deeply, because we are caught up in the larger story of God.

God calls us to move beyond the silence of Adam. We are to abandon ourselves to God with absolute confidence in his goodness; and with the freedom created by that confidence, we are to move into the depths of dangerous uncertainty with a life-giving word. That kind of movement might be something as simple as encouraging a child by giving extra attention, or something as terrifying as giving your heart where it may not be wanted.

But that is where the rub is in moving beyond Adam's silence: we experience fear. A commitment to manly movement *creates* healthy fear. We realize there is no code to follow in the arenas we determine to enter. But it also creates a sense of anticipation. As we resolve to speak in darkness, God gives courage: not the sort that stills trembling legs but the kind that helps us move forward on them.

It's an interesting progression. When men move forward in faith, they more deeply realize their need for God, and therefore more earnestly seek him. And when we seek him with all our hearts, we find him. That's the promise.

Men who spend their lives finding God are quietly transformed from mere men into elders: *godly men* who know what it means to trust a person when there is no plan to follow; *spiritual fathers* who enter dark caves that their children run from; *Christlike mentors* who speak into that darkness with strength instead of control, with gentleness instead of destructive force, and with wisdom that cuts through the confusion to the beauty beyond.

The path to authentic manhood is entered through the narrow gate of a single-minded passion to abandon oneself completely to God. The path beyond the gate is the freedom to speak into darkness as one hears and echoes the voice of a well-remembered God.

PART 2

Something Vital Is Missing

The Problems of Masculine Community

If a man is honest with himself at the exact moment he feels most threatened, he will admit to feeling terror and self-doubt. At that point, rather than abandoning himself to Christ in humility and faith, and leaving explanations and guarantees behind, he is more likely to ask a self-absorbing question for which there is only one discouraging answer: "Do I have what it takes to handle whatever it is I find threatening?" He therefore lives in fear, desperately determined to avoid exposure of his inadequacy. He gives little thought to what it would mean to give of himself as a man.

Men generally live without a clear vision for what masculine movement into life—especially into relationships—would look like. They have lost the joy of dreaming. When you lose contact with Christ, you can no longer dream noble dreams.

Chapter 8

Men Who Fight the Darkness

Pleasant. That's what he was. Kind. Thoughtful. Respectful. Concerned to honor God in every way, especially in his treatment of women.

He would turn forty in two months. Still single. Nothing wrong with that. The apostle Paul seemed to think it a higher calling. It wasn't that he didn't want to marry or that he had a problem with the opposite sex. And he certainly had no homosexual leanings.

The right girl simply hadn't come along. He knew he had high standards. Was that so wrong? If some of his friends had had higher standards, they wouldn't be in the middle of so many marriage problems today.

Maybe *this* singles group would be God's place of provision. He had to admit there were lots of good women in the other three—but maybe they were all involved with the wrong churches. Doctrine was important to him. Now that he was older, he could see more clearly. The three churches since college—that was more than fifteen years ago—were each off base on something important.

He could see it now: the first was too charismatic, although that had appealed to him when he was younger; the second, too legalistic; the third, well, just a bit too "high church"—too much liturgy.

Now that he was in the right church, maybe God would provide the right partner. He would wait and see—and pray, of course.

The last woman—great lady, attractive, godly. And very available—but for the wrong reason. Married before. He wasn't sure it was sinful to marry a divorced woman, but he really did want to keep his standards high. Broke it off just before he weakened enough to propose. Close call. He thanked God for the strength to back away.

And the two women before her. (There were only three he steadily dated. A few fix-ups along the way, but no real possibilities.) One liked him—they seemed to really click. Then suddenly she cooled off. Said something about feeling "missed" by him; they just stopped connecting. Told him he was pleasant, like a casual friend. She wanted more. Probably immature. A girl after fun and excitement. Wanted Prince Charming to ride in on a white horse and sweep her off her feet. Well, he wanted his wife to have her feet on the ground, to be someone who lived to serve Christ even when the excitement wasn't there.

Then the one before her—his first real love. That's what he thought then. But looking back, he now knew it was puppy love. Dated for eight years. She got tired of waiting. He wanted to make sure it was God's will. Nothing worse than moving ahead of God. She was too impulsive.

Time to leave for the singles fellowship. Better pray first, for God's blessing—new friends, encouragement, maybe the right girl. Why did that old man's comment come back to his mind now? Right while he was praying. It was more than five months ago. What was his name? Stevens. Mr. Stevens. Retired. Said he wanted to meet for coffee. He asked so many questions. Never in a pushy way, but with an intense sort of purpose.

And then that sentence. Well, a couple of them. How did he put it? "I hope you'll forgive me if I'm being rude, but I want to say something to you. I don't think your approach to women is very manly. I think you want them to pursue you, like a high school boy hoping a pretty girl asks you to dance."

That image—of him standing to the side, waiting for a girl to pursue him . . . he couldn't get it out of his mind. It stung when Mr. Stevens first said it. Now it just lingered, like an old injury.

Well, he'd just have to wait on God to show him what he should do.

Men who ask "What should I do?" are often asking another question, a far more disturbing one: "Do I have what it takes to do what a real man is called by God to do?" That question, of course, stays undercover. It makes us too uncomfortable. But it's there; we can't completely hide from it.

Men were designed to remember God and to move with courage into regions where there is no code. Because we were designed that way, something feels out of whack when we play it safe. And we know it. Every time we back away from something that we're too scared to face, we sense that something's not right. But we're too scared to explore what's wrong.

We manage to dull the sense that something's wrong; we learn to live with a mildly troubled conscience. But the urge to play it safe, when we yield to it, causes problems. It weakens us in other areas.

Sometimes it releases other urges that are too strong to resist. A fantasy life that won't quit. Perverted desires that we can't shake. Men who forget God often develop resentment toward their wives for being dull, overweight, or unappreciative. The resentment may fuel sexual demands or smother sexual interest. It may lead to late-night pornography in a hotel room or to compulsive masturbation or to adultery.

We like to blame sexual struggles on too much sex drive or on crazy backgrounds that crossed some sexual wires or on uncooperative wives. Or we insist that the problem is simply disobedience to God and that the solution is more time on our knees and in the Word, coupled with a stronger commitment to sexual purity.

It is true that each of these elements may be involved in a man's struggle with sex. Certainly the choice to disobey is involved in every act of sexual sin.

But beneath *obvious* sin there may be *hidden* sin: an even more serious but less-noticed failure than looking at pornography; a sin that weakens and deceives us to the point where the choice to yield to immoral urges seems reasonable, even necessary. Like an undiagnosed tumor that causes headaches, our deeper sin will continue to bear its immoral fruit until it is recognized and dealt with.

The root problem beneath our more visible problems is that we don't strive for depth or quality in our relationships. We're not richly masculine as husbands, fathers, sons, brothers, or friends. We steer clear of those areas in our relationships that utterly baffle us, because we don't want to accept our responsibility to move without a code. Any situation that demands we move with courage confronts us with the dreaded question "Do I have what it takes to do what a real man is called by God to do?"

Sexual health cannot exist without relational health, and relational health requires us to travel down a path that turns in ways we cannot predict.

Part 1 of this book looked at the energy behind the question "What should I do?" We discussed the demand for a code, the refusal to speak into darkness, the determination to live within the sphere of management and thereby not fail, the choice to forget God, the "reasonable" yearning to make it in life without exercising the deepest kind of courage, the paralyzing urge to be like Adam and keep silent when words are called for. Something serious is wrong with men—and it is our silence.

In part 2 ("Something Vital Is Missing") we take a closer look at the fear beneath the demand that life work as it should—the fear expressed in the question "Do I have what it takes to do what a real man is called by God to do?" We pay special attention to

—how we handle that fear (chapter 8)
—two kinds of relating typical of unmanly men (chapter 9)
—men who demand that others come through for them (chapter 10)
—men who need only themselves (chapter 11)

First, then, what do men do when they feel the fear of moving into a situation they have no idea how to handle?

In this world, nobody can avoid the darkness. We are all caught in situations that stump us. And usually those situations involve unexpected problems in our relationships.

A good friend of mine, whom I'll call "Chad," is a man whose masculinity I deeply respect. He woke up one Monday morning to the noise of a slammed door. He jumped out of bed and pulled back the curtains in time to see "Scotty," his teenage son, walking hurriedly away from their house, obviously distressed.

Chad looked at the clock on the nightstand. It was 6:10—the sun was barely up.

Immediately my friend panicked. Something was obviously wrong. He didn't know what it was. Should he pull on his pants and run after Scotty? Should he drop to his knees and pray? His wife, a sound sleeper, hadn't heard the noise. She was still asleep. Should he wake her, Chad wondered?

In the few seconds it required to feel thoroughly confused, he felt his anger growing. This was *not* the way he planned to begin the new week. The anger, he noticed, was directed toward his son. Scotty had been acting strange for more than a month—and he wouldn't talk about it. Come to think of it, ever since he was little, Scotty had been a source of frustration. Always one step out of line with the family.

Then, without warning, the hostility shifted. Chad now felt mad at himself. Had he not spent enough time with his oldest boy? The demands of work had multiplied over the past several years. Family devotions, even family outings, had become more infrequent. Even his wife had mentioned how preoccupied he was with work, but she never complained. Maybe she was too scared of him to be honest.

Were things far worse than Chad thought? Was his marriage in trouble? Was Scotty on drugs? Scotty *had* seemed more irritable lately. His grades had slipped. He was staying in his room more. That is, the little time he spent at home.

What was that article Chad read in the paper last week about teenage suicide? *What was happening* to his son, to his family, to him?

Now his mind was racing. It was just five minutes since the door had slammed, and he was having a nervous breakdown. He wanted to wake up his wife and yell at her—about something, anything. He wanted to run after Scotty and shake some sense into that fool kid's head. No! That would make things worse. Maybe he could take Scotty to breakfast for a real father-son talk; go in late to work. Spend time with his boy. That sounded good.

Chad told himself to stay calm and get a grip. After all, his whole family were Christians—grandparents included, on both sides. God would make it all work out right. He needed more faith. God could be trusted.

But the assistant pastor's daughter—pregnant at age sixteen. Was that working out right? And that missionary couple they prayed for a year ago—their only son had taken his life. Had they not trusted God? Is that why the tragedy happened? Bad things happened in Christian homes, better homes than his. That was obvious. And Sid, his racquetball partner—his son, in his early twenties, missing for two years. Dead? On drugs? Too filled with hate to call his parents? Sid didn't know.

God, what have you promised? What can I depend on? What is predictable? *What should I do?*

That's the first question men ask.

Suppose, in reply to that question, Chad heard a firm voice say, "Be a man. Decide what best reflects the character of God and move accordingly. Be courageous. Be wise. Be imaginative. You love God. You love your son. Do something!"

Most men have heard that voice, sometimes through an older, wiser man. I have. "But what should I do?" we ask again. There *has* to be a code. There has to be an expert who knows what someone should do in every situation. It's okay to be confused, but not totally. Dusk is one thing. Midnight darkness is another.

God knows what we should do. Surely *he* will tell us. And then we realize—the voice was his. He *is* telling us what to do, but it's not a code. He tells us to be men, to love him, and then to do whatever we think is best. Adam came up with names for all the animals without any prompting from God. God didn't whisper suggestions ("See if you think 'ostrich' fits that long-necked bird over there") or make corrections ("No, no! 'Hippopotamus' doesn't sound right for that one. 'Rabbit' works far better").

When it finally dawns on us that God is waiting for us to move and to speak into darkness, that his instruction is to choose a direction consistent with what we know of him, then we stop asking the first question. We have to. He simply won't tell us specifically what to do. We begin to face the loneliness of choice, the terror of trust.

That's when the second question arises from parts deep within us, accompanied by a level of fear that leaves us feeling more alone than ever before: "Do I have what it takes to do what God calls a man—a manly man—to do? If I move, will it be with wisdom? Do I have the courage to do something with absolutely no guarantees other than that God's ultimate purposes will be achieved? Am I willing to move into the mystery of relationship with another human being, renouncing all efforts to control the outcome?"

In all their days, very few men touch even one other human being with a word that brings life-giving freedom. We're simply too afraid to face what might happen if a wife, a son or daughter, or a friend slipped out from under our control and stepped forward in his or her unpredictable individuality.

If we really choose to enter the unpredictability of relationships, we're not at all sure that we can speak a word of life. And we're not sure if we want people to make their own choices as they relate to us. Can we handle what might happen if people close to us actually were freed?

Better to keep women in their place and children quietly obedient, less heard than seen. And men too. Friendships continue more smoothly if certain topics are avoided. Real relating asks too much of us. We can handle nodding acquaintances.

When God confronts you with a relational situation so confusing and important that you cry out the words "God, I want to be a man. But do I have what it takes?" Then rejoice. You are standing at a gate that opens to the narrow path of true masculine godliness.

It is a gate that few men ever open. And for good reason. No amount of force can open it. The gate never swings open to a man who approaches it with the confidence of one who is used to making things happen. Only a man who has left the sphere of management—one who has fallen prostrate before mystery but desperately longs to enter it—will, in his weakness, be strong enough to open it.

No man who carries his own light into the darkness will ever set foot on the path to manhood. Listen to the words of Isaiah:

> Let him who walks in the dark, who has no light, trust in the name of the LORD and rely on his God.
>
> But now, all you who light fires and provide yourselves with flaming torches, go, walk in the light of your fires and of the torches you have set ablaze.
>
> This is what you shall receive from my hand: You will lie down in torment. (Isaiah 50:10–11)

Lighting our own fires is another way of describing what men do when they find themselves in a dark place. They scramble back to something they can manage, perhaps redefining the confusion into a more understandable and therefore controllable package. They depend on recipe theology, looking for an expert to supply a code that tells them what to do in order to guarantee a desired result.

They refuse to move into the darkness with only the confidence that God is with them.[1]

Suppose my friend who was awakened by the noise of a slammed door had responded to his frantic concerns without humbling himself. Suppose he had never faced up to what was going on inside of him: the anger, the self-reproach, the terror filling his heart. Suppose he had kept his distance from all that he felt, and instead had decided to figure out what needed to be done and then had done it. He would have never been broken by his pride, never been undone by his insistence that he must always know what to do, never been repentant over his self-centered demand that the important things in his life must operate according to a plan under his control.

If Chad had never gone deep enough into his heart to be broken by his arrogance and humbled by his impotence, then *whatever* choice he would have made that Monday morning would have been a lighting of his own fire. Let me put it plainly: Whenever our highest agenda is to make our lives work, then no matter what we do, we are fire-lighters.

But when our highest agenda is to love Christ, to please him and represent him well to others, then whatever action we take will involve reliance and trust "in the name of the Lord." If we really do love Christ, then of course our choices will be made within the boundaries clearly laid down in Scripture. We may wake our wives, but we will not yell at them. We may *not* wake our wives, but we will not later scorn them for sleeping through a family crisis. Waking or not waking our wives is a choice we are free to make. Taking out our frustrations on them is clearly forbidden. And when a godly man does what is wrong, when he walks outside of the light God has given, he owns his mistake, he accepts full blame, and he asks forgiveness.

Chad is a godly man. Listen to what it meant for him to move into darkness without lighting his own fire. He admitted to himself how impatient, self-reproachful, and irritable he felt. He consciously yielded himself to God as a weak man who did not know what to do, reminding himself that the chosen purpose of his entire life, including that moment Monday morning, was to love Christ and to honor him in all he did.

He still felt mad and scared. But his heart and will were set as firmly as his level of maturity allowed. His faith felt weak; but perhaps, he thought, it neared the size of a mustard seed.

He thought for a minute and decided not to wake his wife but to quickly dress, go downstairs, sit on the front step, and wait for his son to return. The image that guided him was the prodigal's father, not searching for his son in a foreign land but waiting eagerly for his return. Maybe the passage didn't apply. Maybe the parable of the Lord going after the one lost sheep should lead him to go looking for his son. He couldn't be sure. There was no light; only darkness. But he was trusting God as best he knew. He made a decision even when he wasn't sure what to do. He moved; he moved into mystery.

The point of the story is *not* what happened next. Whether he later received news that his son had killed himself or whether he welcomed him home within minutes is clearly a matter of heart-stopping significance. *But the outcome of the story does not determine whether my friend acted like a man.*

Whatever occurred next that Monday morning would require more "decisions of trust," more speaking into darkness, more movement without a code. Had Scotty taken his life, decisions involving Chad's unspeakable pain would have been necessary, perhaps beginning with the decision to let others minister to him during a long season of healing.

Had his son returned home but stormed past his father into the house, a different set of decisions would have been required. Had Scotty returned in tears, eager to pour out his heart, even then my friend would have needed to make decisions. What questions should he ask, if any? Should he just listen? Offer advice? Pray?

Once we become Christians, our most important decisions are often made in the darkness, with only God's light. We must trust a God who often does not tell us exactly what to do. The Spirit more often whispers *encouragement* ("You can do it. I am with you") than *directions* ("Now go tell her this"). We must develop a relationship with Christ in which we come to know him well enough to behave like he would, to sense what he would do, what he might say. We must honor our calling to reflect his habit of moving through darkness toward beauty.

God calls on men to speak into darkness that sometimes stays dark, even after we speak. We must not search for a flashlight to shine on the path. When we insist on knowing what to do in trying to achieve our goals, we are fire-lighters.

Lighting our own fires is a natural tendency in every fallen man. And that tendency is clearly visible, not only in the relational crises of life but also in our everyday style of relating. Men who routinely light fires rather than trust God reveal their lack of manliness most significantly in the way they engage other people, particularly women. It is to these unmanly patterns of relating that we turn in the next three chapters.

---

1 The Isaiah passage, of course, applies to women every bit as much as to men. Any approach to life that doesn't center in trust eventually produces misery.

OF ADAM

Chapter 9

The Way Unmanly Men Relate

Funny how *unchosen* self-awareness could feel. He had faced hard things about himself before. At age eight, the idea that he was a sinner became clear. But he hadn't arranged for that insight. It just happened. Choice was mixed in there somehow, but it felt more arranged *for* him than *by* him.

Maybe he was too self-aware. Some thought him introspective, occasionally morbid, too preoccupied with his motives and feelings. But others commended him for it. They spoke of his openness and vulnerability.

Their admiration had worn thin. If one more person admiringly told him how "real" he was, he thought he might get sick. Realness didn't feel like a big virtue; it felt more like a small part of his calling—as inevitable, and perhaps as necessary, as breathing.

This latest episode of self-discovery had crept up on him. It never really climaxed in one bright burst of light or one anguished descent into brokenness. It just kept slowly coming, like a trickle from years ago that was now a flowing river, gradually pushing its way into his mind.

Was he really that petty, that selfishly immature? Did he really grasp after approval like an infant groping for milk? The evidence was in the small things, sometimes in honest feedback from others about his effect on them; sometimes, like this time, the evidence came in routine happenings that unexpectedly brought his pattern into clear focus.

It was just last week. He had gone to bed early, exhausted, maybe coming down with a cold. He had read for a few minutes, then turned out the light. About an hour had passed. He had just fallen asleep.

His wife, catching up on a few responsibilities in another part of the house, heard a noise. She felt frightened. Out of reflex, she called his name once . . . and then again, this time standing outside the bedroom door, speaking loud enough to wake him.

Before he could respond, his wife recognized the source of the noise. It was the wind blowing through an open window. No cause for alarm. She said, "Everything's okay." Then she apologized: "I'm sorry I woke you."

Some men would have growled, "Can't I get some extra sleep in my own house?" Some would have mumbled, wanting only to get back to sleep. Good men would have felt concern for their wives, neither growling nor mumbling. Their wives would have felt wanted rather than bothersome.

As he returned his head to the pillow, he felt two things. First, *encouraged*. He had felt warm toward his wife; he had not snapped at her or made incoherent noises. He knew he had meant it when he had replied to her apology by saying, "That's okay. You were scared." He didn't feel proud, just encouraged. Second, he felt *sobered*. He realized the familiar demons had not been cast out; and although they might have been bound, they had not been gagged. He had heard them cackle their seductive message: "Things never really go right for you. The first night in months that you've gone to bed early. You'd think somebody would notice how tired you are and care about it. That's not asking too much; that's only asking for what you want but never get—someone who puts you first. You've come through for a lot of people. Is it so wrong to ask that someone come through for you?"

He lay there, wanting to stuff dirty rags in every demon's mouth. But he felt grateful that he had listened to a better voice, and he was more aware than ever that the real battle he must fight was within himself, against an enemy that pretended to be a friend.

Charlie's job was not going well. The new director of operations, a thoroughly arrogant self-appointed messiah, was making his life at work miserable. Charlie was discouraged, maybe even depressed. His wife was genuinely supportive. He appreciated that.

But sometimes he felt like such a weight on her. What did she really think of him? How would she react when he came home feeling low— again? Maybe he talked about his problems too much. But he couldn't pretend he was up. He just couldn't be breezy and cheerful when he felt like this. All the way home, he pondered how best to handle his wife.

Mark was different. His job was as big a mess as Charlie's. But he'd deal with it. Mark's wife could tell when things at work weren't going so well for him; he became even more sure of himself, even less reflective. She would ask him how he felt. "No problems" was Mark's favorite response. Then would come a stream of criticism: "The new management hasn't got a clue about what would make our company really fly. Jenkins, that new guy, is a real turkey. He doesn't like me and I don't like him. But it'll all work out, one way or another."

That would be it. Case closed. Door shut. Dinner conversation would be pleasant for the most part, except for a few sharp jabs at the kids, and one or two directed toward her. And then television for three hours.

Line up a hundred men. Watch them closely for one week. With only a little discernment, you will recognize one of two patterns in their dealings with people. Seventy or eighty will be ruled by a passion called neediness. Something inside them needs attention. The chosen few on whom they deeply depend are required to think about them and treat them in a certain way. They are more than willing to do their part, to do the right thing, but their goal is always the same: to get something from another person. Charlie fits in this group, which I will label Pattern 1.

The other twenty or thirty will be ruled by a very different passion. The passion that controls their behavior, especially their behavior in personal relationships, is not neediness. Rather it is toughness: a proud, "I don't need you or anybody else" sort of attitude. Mark belongs to this second group, which I will call Pattern 2.

In their relational styles, men are generally ruled by one of these two passions. Either they are controlled by the *passion of neediness*, which says "Come through for me! Fill me—I'm empty!" or they operate according to the *passion of toughness*, where the message is "I can handle things without you. Believe in me from a distance, and don't give me any hassles."

Let me first suggest why these two patterns are basic and why most men fit into one of them, and then in Chapter 10 I'll discuss the first pattern. In Chapter 11 we'll take a look at the second.

WHY MEN MOVE ONE WAY OR THE OTHER

God wants everyone happy—not on our terms, which never really bring happiness, but on his. Like an owner's manual for a new car, his terms require that we use the plans specifically drawn up for us.

No man can be happy unless he is living out his calling to be a man. Exciting but shallow pleasures, the kind that do not require us to worry about some deep call to manhood, may disguise themselves as true happiness. Power, influence, money, status, connections, achievement, success, possessions, food, sex, recreation: lots of things, many of them good in their place, get defined as the source of happiness. And the tricky thing is that they do keep their promise—or at least seem to—for varying periods of time, occasionally for years. They make us feel good; they do something for us.

But they don't really do the job. They do not produce a contentment that survives loss, a joy that deepens through suffering, a humble confidence that persists through failure and setback.

By going after these sources of pleasure, we reduce ourselves to puppets, supported by strings that—if cut—leave us in a heap on the ground.

No man can be happy without living out the call to make visible that which is hard to see about God. Happiness comes for a man when he shows, by his life, that God is always moving, is never stopped by darkness, and is continually up to something good, no matter how bad things may appear.

Men are called to hover over darkness, to enter the mystery of relationships until they are humbled enough to trust God, and then to act to further God's purposes. That action, by the way, will fall flat with a loud thud unless God is in it. Most men never even think like this; they never give their call from God a moment's thought. And not even the best man lives out his manhood completely.

If it is true that no man can be completely happy without perfectly honoring God's call to be a man, then it follows that no man on earth is completely happy. Every one of us struggles with some measure of unhappiness, some experience of internal emptiness and restless dissatisfaction, that our Creator never intended for us to endure.

From deep within our hearts, in those places of our being that we do not understand, a yearning emerges. It is a desperate longing for a response, a vacuum that needs to be filled. It is also an angry turbulence that won't let us sit still. To at least some degree, every man knows that he is not fully happy. And when his unfulfilled desires surface into the light of day, he is confronted with the essential choice of human existence: to trust God or not to trust him, to light his own fires or to rely on the name of the Lord.

If he trusts God, the unhappiness (which must continue till death) is surrounded by hope, by acceptance, by meaning in spite of imperfection. And he is empowered to move well. That brings joy.

If he refuses to trust, the unhappiness within him becomes his most compelling problem. He must find some way to deal with it.

We must understand a simple principle: every man is moving. Movement defines a man's existence. But all movement is not good. Therefore, when a man is not moving as he should, he will move in ways he should not. *When good movement stops, bad movement begins.* Good movement is movement through personal unhappiness toward God. Bad movement is movement aimed at nothing higher than relieving personal unhappiness.

Because men, like women, are fundamentally relational beings, all movement will be seen most clearly in the way a man relates. A man will either call forth life and beauty in the people he knows or he will destroy that same life and beauty. A man's effect on others may be imperceptible or dramatic, but it is there. No interaction of more than a few seconds, no conversation beyond the most casual, leaves the other person unchanged.

Manly men release others from their control and encourage them with their influence. They touch their wives, children, and friends in sensitive ways that free them to struggle with *their* loneliness and selfishness and pain. Manly men nudge their family and friends to the same crossroads where they, as men, have found that trust or unbelief must be chosen.

Unmanly men require their friends and family to meet their demands. Men who move with control, anger, and terror deaden others into conformity or incite them to self-preserving rebellion.

WHY PATTERN I

Unmanly men who practice the first pattern of bad movement in relationship, who insist others come through for them, understand that happiness can never be found in isolation, only in community. Their background usually includes someone who brought them intense pleasure: perhaps a doting mother, a too-generous father, an overly solicitous (maybe inappropriately involved) youth pastor, or an admired athlete who gave his autograph. As boys, these men learned a simple lesson: internal pain is most reliably relieved when someone does something for them.

A strategy takes shape in the mind of a Pattern 1 thinker, a strategy that accommodates his inclination not to move in ways that could reveal his inadequacy: *get others to respond to my needs without requiring good movement from me.* Now he doesn't have to confront his own terror of darkness and his real need for God, and he has hope.

The passion of neediness rules in all the decisions of a man following Pattern 1: to marry or not to marry, this woman or that one; deciding on career moves, choosing activities with friends, determining whether or not to spank his children. That same passion rules in even the smallest decisions. Shall I tell my wife what I feel? Do I go to that party? Should I complain about the service from that waitress?

Like a wealthy man's son depending on monthly checks from his trust fund, a man ruled by his own neediness comes to think it is his right to never have to move on his own. He is willing to be responsible up to a point, and he is often willing to be kind and thoughtful, sometimes even sacrificially helpful, but always with the demand that someone notice—and that someone give him what makes him feel good. That's a Pattern 1 man.

WHY PATTERN 2

Either unmanly men turn to others with a well-managed display of neediness or they push people far enough away from them to avoid any significant sense of connection. Men ruled by the passion of toughness typically have a history more characterized by neglect or anger than by pleasurable involvement. Rigid discipline, preoccupied fathers, nonnurturing mothers, meaningless churches, legalistic theology: relational connection never existed for long in these men's experience.

The men who now act according to Pattern 2 were starving for relationship but they lost hope. It was easier to kill their yearnings for intimacy and get on with life than to embrace their longings and hurt. Admitting how badly they wanted connection became a greater terror for them than the prospect of searching for relationship but never finding it.

Often abilities surfaced that permitted them to find the pleasures of "relationship from a distance." Athletic talent or academic gift or social smoothness or a mechanical knack gave them a chance to feel powerful and to achieve goals worthy of commendation.

Over time, a Pattern 2 man comes to depend on his abilities so fully that his human longing for connection is smothered. And that's how he wants it. Distance maintains safety. No need to feel that soul-crushing terror of needing that which may not come your way.

In one sense, of course, this man is every bit as needy as a man living out Pattern 1. Both unmanly relating styles demand that others come through. But men in touch with their neediness require up close affirmation and support from a few intimates. And "tough" men want respect from a larger audience that keeps its distance. The styles may be different, but both are selfish. And both cause great harm.

One of the great tragedies of life is that no man fully sees the damage that his unmasculine style of relating does to others. Those that get a glimpse descend to the depths of brokenness and contrition.

And it is from those depths that genuine repentance arises. When a broken man repents, the Spirit gives him new vision. A cool stream makes its way into the burning desert of his brokenness. The hope of actually *blessing* others—nourishing his wife, positively influencing his children, encouraging his friends—grows stronger than the terror of entering darkness. And good movement begins.

Good movement never just happens. Nor does it develop naturally; there is always a fight against powerful urges in the other direction. Good movement always begins in repentance over bad movement. And repentance comes after (1) an acknowledgment of wrong, leading to brokenness, and (2) a depth of confession that only humility can create.

In the next two chapters, I discuss these two patterns in more detail. See if you can find yourself somewhere: if not clearly in a story or description, then perhaps between the lines. We're all there.

Chapter 10

Men Who Demand Others Come Through for Them: The Passion of Neediness

The courtship had been stormy. Maybe that was to be expected at their age: she in her mid-thirties, he pushing forty. After so many years of singleness, they'd be set in their ways. They were past the innocence of dreamy idealism. No longer desperate to get married, they were now determined not to make a mistake.

It had been tough. And it was still tough, just three weeks before the big day. But something kept them together. He thought it was love. She wanted to believe that, but she wasn't sure.

Her doubts rose most strongly when she felt put upon. "Sometimes I feel like your mother, like you want me to always be there with milk and cookies when you get home from school. And I hate it! I hate feeling that way!"

The image—herself as his mother—popped into her mind most clearly whenever he expressed hurt over something she had done or had failed to do. He seemed so pathetic, like a lost child. That same image was also evoked, though not quite so strongly, when he complained about fatigue or job stress or health worries. He called it "sharing," or being vulnerable about his struggles. She felt pulled to come through for him.

In a remarkably rare and honest moment, after one more long discussion about her feelings on the matter, he admitted, "I can never struggle without experiencing myself as a child. Whenever I tell you that I'm hurt-. ing, I feel like a little kid. Maybe I do want you to mother me.

"When I really was little, the only time I ever remember feeling tenderness from my mother was when I was hurting."

He teared up. There was a long pause. A memory flashed through his mind. "I broke my wrist in fifth grade. Fell off my bike. The bone was sticking up through my skin. The doctor had to reset it. I was scared to death. I can picture Mother standing next to my bed in the emergency room. I never felt so protected, so cared for. I could see it in her eyes."

He sobbed.

She felt an urge to touch him. But that mother image came again. And it made her urge to touch him feel unclean.

Seconds passed. A minute. He stopped crying and looked up. "Did you feel it just now? Like my mother? Like I wanted you to take care of me?"

She hesitated, then quietly said, "Yes. I wish I didn't."

His eyes were instantly dry. He stared at her, bewildered and enraged. He nearly shouted, "Is it so wrong to want my fiancée to feel a little of my pain? Does that make you my mother? Can't a man ever want his woman just to be there for him?"

More tears. Now they were both crying. They felt frustrated; they sensed the darkness.

"What are we going to do?" she asked.

"I don't know," he answered.

Unmanly men live to get what they think they need. Unmanly men driven by the passion of neediness try to get it from others.

One woman said to me, "When I hear my husband's car pull in the driveway after work, my heart just sinks. I immediately feel even more tired than I felt before. I'm a housewife with three little kids to take care of all day. And now here comes a fourth."

"What does he do that makes you feel that way?" I asked. He was sitting next to her, managing to scowl and look hurt at the same time.

"A thousand things," she replied. "It could be a sigh when he walks in the door or a comment about traffic on the way home. Sometimes he tells me how tired he feels. It could be anything. But it's always about him, about something that's wrong, like I'm supposed to do something. Even when he asks about me, I feel set up to ask about him. If he helps with dinner, I get that look that tells me I'm supposed to tell him how wonderful he is.

"And if I do something special for him, even something little, like a really affectionate greeting, he's too appreciative. It makes me feel like he really needed it, that I better keep on giving it to him, or he'll be really hurt. Sometimes when he's extra thoughtful, I think he's telling me I better be available for sex, but lots of time it's not that. I don't know how else to put it—everything he does makes me feel that I'm supposed to come through for him."

Many needy men hide their neediness better than this woman's husband. They may be far more subtle and "manly" in their expression of need. And every one of us follows the pattern of tough men or needy men at various points in our lives. There is no such thing as a pure Pattern 1 or Pattern 2 man. But one pattern often becomes a theme in our style of relating.

A man who typically follows the first pattern lives his life thinking others should come through for him. His sense of neediness is so real, so deep, so compelling, that asking for understanding or attention seems entirely reasonable to him. His life depends on getting it. The Pattern 1 man defines himself by his neediness, just as some men today define themselves by their homosexual inclinations. For homosexual men, not to "come out" and express their urges feels like a betrayal of their identity, a violation of something basic within them that belongs to their essential nature. So too with men whose neediness feels core to their being. They feel most comfortable and alive when someone is taking care of them. More than anything else, they see themselves as needy. And someone should do something about it.

When they feel let down, when someone does not come through as required, men who define themselves by their needs feel they have been profoundly failed. Justice has miscarried. Rights have been denied. The human community has been inhuman.

The effect, of course, is anger. Resentment boils up, and it feels justified. And with justified resentment comes justified revenge. Think how easily sarcastic comments pour through our lips. We lash out with remarks that cut. Perhaps we inflict only small wounds, like paper cuts—but they hurt. That, of course, is the intent. To hurt the one who failed to come through.

Men ruled by the passion of neediness get even: if not with sarcasm and cuts, then with irritability or grumpiness or indifference. Wives who fail need-driven men are made to pay. So are the friends of these men.

But needy men don't see the damage they inflict. In their eyes, they are the failed ones, not their wives and friends. A needy man confronted with his cruelty reacts often like a starving beggar caught stealing a loaf of bread. "Look, maybe what I did was wrong. I'm sure it was. But you've got to understand what I've been through. Given how hungry I am, I'm really not asking for much."

One man made a habit of cruising a red-light district, occasionally picking up a prostitute or indulging in a peep show, all the time persuading himself that his sin was not nearly so wicked as the way his family sinned against him while he was growing up and the way his wife was failing him now.

Twenty-five years of counseling experience makes me guess that nine men in ten feel more troubled by the way others let them down than by how they hurt others. And married men are especially troubled by the ways their wives fail them.

Men ruled by neediness benefit from the fact that our culture is committed to not blaming the victim. For example, when a parent neglects a baby boy, we do not hold the infant responsible for either the parent's failure or the damage that failure caused. We support the child in his pain and do all that we can to protect him from further harm.

But we have carried our protection of the victim too far. We have denied the responsibility of adult victims to suffer gracefully and to continue doing good. We have allowed the severity of other people's wrongs against us to blind us to God's unchanging call to be holy. As the little boy victimized by parental neglect matures, we must be careful to encourage him to develop an identity built around the opportunities of manhood, not around his pain and neediness.

But developing that kind of identity requires the work of the Holy Spirit. No one naturally thinks of himself as an image-bearer whose highest calling is to reflect the character of an unseen God. There are more urgent matters pressing for attention, like getting what we need to survive and what we need to survive more comfortably. Men facing bankruptcy usually expend more effort in figuring out how to pay their bills than in learning to know God.

No amount of damage from others, and no circumstance of life, can ever destroy the image of God within us or nullify the call to bear that image well, but we tend to think otherwise. Pain speaks so loudly that we have a hard time hearing God's call to live like men. Violating God's image by unethical business dealings or by seducing another man's wife can actually feel like a small thing. We all struggle with things that just don't seem very bad, especially when we're feeling particularly let down.

Only when the Spirit of God, through his Word, exposes the heart's thoughts and attitudes will any of us see clearly. Only then will the ruling passion of neediness be recognized for what it is: a sinful basis for relating to others that is not worthy of men.

THE EXAMPLE OF SAUL

King Saul is perhaps the Bible's premier example of a need-driven man who, as always happens when needs rule our lives, lost his dignity. One incident from many that could be chosen will make the point. Read 1 Samuel 15 for the whole story that I will now summarize.

One day Saul committed a particularly grievous sin that caused God to reject him as king. In conversation with Samuel shortly after his sin, Saul denied any wrongdoing. Notice carefully that at this point, while he still thought his sin had gone unnoticed, he claimed that he had not been disobedient.

"I have carried out the Lord's instructions," he proudly announced to Samuel. Those instructions included killing every living thing that belonged to the Amalekites, a nation whose complete destruction God had decreed. In fact, Saul had spared the Amalekite king, a man named Agag, and he had not slaughtered all the livestock, deciding rather to save the best cows and sheep (for sacrifice to the Lord, according to his later testimony).

In an almost amusing passage, Samuel replies to Saul's declaration of complete obedience, asking, "What then is this bleating of sheep in my ears? What is this lowing of cattle that I hear?"

Saul was caught. He could no longer deny his disobedience. He had not destroyed everything. And so he changed his tune from denial to what—at first glance—looks like confession: "I have sinned. I violated the Lord's command."

But the rest of the story makes clear that Saul's acknowledgment of sin did not come out of brokenness. Saul was scrambling, looking for a way to avoid God's judgment and to keep at least the perks of his job as king. He clearly illustrates the truth that without brokenness over sin, there can be neither genuine confession nor sincere repentance.

Saul does not exhibit a broken and contrite spirit. Far from it. Rather he begs Samuel to return to the capital city and to stand with him in public worship, hoping that Samuel's presence would grant Saul some measure of continued respect as king.

But Samuel remained adamant. "I will not go back with you. . . . The Lord has rejected you as king over Israel!"

Now, notice carefully what Saul does next, driven entirely by his sense of desperate neediness: "As Samuel turned to leave, Saul caught hold of the hem of his robe, and it tore. Samuel said to him, 'The Lord has torn the kingdom of Israel from you today and has given it to one of your neighbors—to one better than you. . . .' Saul replied, 'I have sinned. But please honor me before the elders of my people and before Israel; come back with me, so that I may worship the Lord your God.'"[1]

The passion of neediness becomes a ruling passion when it is perceived as stronger and more urgent than a passion for holiness. "If I could only have _____" becomes the guiding ambition behind everything a needy man does.

The principle highlighted by Saul's life is important to recognize: a heightened sense of need, if unaccompanied by an even greater sense of sin, justifies and strengthens selfishness. People more aware of their neediness than their sinfulness are people who manipulate and demand. People more aware of their sinfulness repent and develop a ruling passion for holiness. Only these people learn to rest in God's love and to enjoy his favor.

Nearly thirty years of marriage have made it clear to me that I tend more toward this style of relating than the one I will discuss in the next chapter. I often feel more needy than tough. When I am hurt, I'm inclined to see my need for comfort as an opportunity for someone else to do good. The call to rise above my neediness, entrust myself to God, and do good to others is sometimes hard to hear. The deeper the hurt, the less I tend to hear it.

When the passion of neediness rules, no amount of comfort quite does the job. Needy men might thank their wives for their efforts, but with no more enthusiasm than a man who needs a hundred dollars thanks a friend for giving him a quarter.

Whatever mood of gratitude exists gives way quickly to picky criticism: "I don't know why you had to keep working on dinner while I was telling you about our money problems. Is it too much to ask for one minute of your full attention?"

The person who takes on the job of meeting a needy man's needs has no hope of success. No effort is enough. No kindness is sufficient. People in relationship with a Pattern 1 man typically feel

1. the pressure to come through
2. bad that they never come through adequately

Eventually the pressure and the guilt become overwhelming. It may take twenty or thirty years. Then they quit trying. "Why bother? Nothing I do ever satisfies him." The frustration of relating to a Pattern 1 man is often the reason behind the end of a long-term friendship or marriage.

Those who keep on trying to meet a needy man's needs feel more and more worn down, until depression sets in. A needy man's wife finds herself dreaming of a better relationship, one in which she is noticed and appreciated. She begins to notice other men, how they treat their wives, how they treat her. She becomes vulnerable to the slightest hint of affection.

"He seems to enjoy me."

Sometimes romance novels or soap operas provide relief. Sometimes it's busyness: more ministry, more hours at work, more social clubs, more housework, more education.

Women married to needy men feel lonely and scared. They often feel disgusted with themselves. Many hide their pain beneath competence. They become tough and hard, unable to worship or relax or laugh.

Listen to the cry of a needy man: "Come through for me! Don't you know how empty I am, how desperate I feel, how painful my life is? Why can't you

— be more considerate?	— lose weight?
— speak more kindly?	— be more supportive?
— read more books?	— cook more creatively?
— ask me more questions?	— pursue me in bed?
— dress more attractively?	— spend less money?
— talk less at parties?	— be more like her?
— appreciate me more?	— criticize me less?"

A man wrote me a letter in response to a book I had written. "You didn't answer the one question I need to have answered, the one I assumed you'd deal with in your book. I want to know why some women just won't take care of themselves. I'm a millionaire several times over, I'm an elder in our church, I let her buy anything she wants, I'm not a workaholic, and I've never cheated on her.

"What I want to know is: why won't my wife lose weight? I keep myself in good shape. But she won't exercise. She's put on forty pounds in the last two years. I find her as appealing as a bowl of gelatin. I even told her I'd go to counseling with her and look at wherever I might be failing. I just don't get it. What's wrong with women like my wife?"

Like most men ruled by the passion of neediness, this man

1. finds no fault in himself
2. sees only what another could do differently
3. feels justified in his anger
4. cannot see beyond his needs to hers

Because he is blinded by his neediness, the quality of relationship he offers his wife is poor. But he does not see that. Whatever struggles he may have with sexual temptation are thought to be the result of the way he has been treated. In his mind, his efforts to remain sexually clean are noble and require nothing more of him than increased time in the Word and on his knees. It never occurs to him that he is not loving his wife as he should be, that he really isn't much of a man, that he has never learned to speak with love into the confusion and pain of relationship.

When we are ruled by the passion of neediness and believe that our deepest joy lies in others coming through for us, we destroy life and tarnish beauty. At that point, we are not manly men.

---

1 It's worth mentioning in passing that Samuel did go back with Saul, but not to honor him. He rather put the Amalekite king Agag to death in order to carry out the command of God that Saul had disobeyed. Saul remained on the throne, but things went from bad to worse until finally he took his own life. They that light their own fires receive one thing from the Lord's hand: they eventually lie down in torment (Isaiah 50:11).

Chapter 11

Men Who Need Only Themselves: The Passion of Toughness

He always seemed to fit. Whatever the gathering—board meeting, dinner party, church social—he was comfortable. He knew the right people, always dressed the part, and with charm and grace, he related easily in any crowd.

He could, at times, be rather opinionated. His better friends, the ones who were with him more often, had seen his self-confidence cross the line into pushiness.

Although his social acquaintances might not have noticed, he was an intensely private man. He rarely spoke about personal struggles and tended to quickly "resolve" whatever relational tensions he couldn't avoid or dismiss. He never explored himself or anyone else. His family felt the impact of his shallow involvement.

Self-awareness was not, of course, among his virtues. If asked to describe himself, he might offhandedly use words like sociable, well-read, successful, good family man, committed Christian. He might even say manly. He would never wonder *why* someone might ask him to describe himself, or invite the questioner to share his or her thoughts.

He did occasionally get emotional: when he came into his wife's hospital room after her mastectomy; at his father's funeral; when he proposed a toast to his daughter and her bridegroom at their wedding reception.

But he never cried. No one had ever seen him break down. Once, his oldest son asked him when he had last openly wept. "Not since I was a kid," he replied disinterestedly, as though the question were "When was the last time you used acne medication?"

He was good to have for a golfing buddy or a business partner. And certainly the right man to have on your side in an argument.

But he was not one with whom you felt inclined to share your heart.

His wife was terribly lonely. But he would never have guessed it. She buried her pain deep beneath the trappings of moderate wealth and beneath the round of "important" activities that social class required. She busied herself with garden clubs, political meetings, the women's ministry council at church, and home redecorating. Her three attractive kids were the bright red bow that nicely topped the well-wrapped package of her life.

As with most "perfect" lives, there was one dirty smudge, one unsightly crease on her surgically smoothed face. *Panic attacks*. Not severe, but troubling.

They tended to hit when she felt out of control. The first one was provoked by her daughter going to college and dating someone her husband considered a lowlife. She spoke calmly with her daughter about her concerns, having convinced herself that the girl would listen to reason. And she did. She ended up marrying a doctor.

Her husband handled the dating crisis with sarcasm—that's when the term "lowlife" had been used.

The attacks had been regular but infrequent, some worse than others. Medication helped. She got the drugs from an internist, a golfing friend of her husband. Her husband had made the appointment for her. He even drove to pick up the first prescription.

In his mind, that settled things. Toothache? See a dentist. Panic attacks? Take a pill. He never talked to her about them, never explored her fears.

Three times she had unburdened herself and admitted how distant she felt from her husband, how unnecessary she felt except as his social and sexual partner. Once to a close friend, who changed the subject. Once to a visiting cousin, a man she barely knew. He was slightly older and seemed so kind. They stayed up late one night. Years of pent-up feelings poured out. He listened. It felt so good. But he never mentioned it again: not a word the next morning, not a single follow-up phone call, not one letter. She wished she had never said a thing.

The third time was two years later, with a woman therapist she met and chatted with at a party. She actually shared very little. But the therapist seemed to pick up on more than what was said. She seemed concerned. Again it felt so good. She considered making a professional appointment, but thought better of it after mentioning the idea to her husband. "What do you need a shrink for?" was all he said.

There was one other time. It was the last night of a week-long Bible conference. The message was about God's love for the lost sheep, the one who felt abandoned with no hope of being found. It got to her.

She disappeared quickly during the closing prayer and walked by herself around the lake. It was quiet, so warm and reassuringly dark, with only the light of a crescent moon, which was reflected on the still water. An overwhelming sense of peace invited the release of her tears in its safety. She fell to the soft grass, buried her head in her hands, and sobbed uncontrollably. The words flowed without restraint from her heart, expressing what had been so long denied. "I can't take it. It just hurts too much. Nobody wants me. My marriage is empty. I'm more alone than I can bear."

She came back to their room past midnight with puffy eyes. He was sitting up in bed, reading. "Where have you been?" he asked. "I've been worried about you."

"Walking. Thinking. Praying. I even cried a little."

"You didn't forget to take your medication, did you?"

"No," she replied, feeling nothing. She got ready for bed.

Nothing more was said. He leaned over to kiss her on the forehead, smiled reassuringly, then turned over and went to sleep.

She was fine the next morning.

In these chapters, I am talking about two kinds of men: those ruled by their neediness and those ruled by their determination to be tough. These two styles of relating are in fact extreme positions at opposite ends of a long continuum. In this chapter, I will discuss tough men.

But it might be good to introduce this discussion by talking for a moment about the continuum. I have not wanted to suggest another "type" theory for categorizing men. I do *not* want men to read this book and say, "Yeah, that's me. I guess that's who I am." I *do* hope that many men will recognize their relational patterns and respond, "That is how I treat my wife (or friends). That's awful. I'm more of a man than that." I want us to grow in masculinity by understanding not only God's design for men but also our ways of corrupting it.

Needy men are corrupted men. They are more inclined to be aware of their thirst for affirmation as they relate to others, and more inclined to enter relationships for no higher reason than to meet their own needs. Tough men are equally but differently corrupted. They deny any deep longing for relationship, and chase after goals that do not require meaningful intimacy with people.

These patterns represent two opposing extremes in how men relate. These are the end points on a long continuum that looks like this:

STYLE OF RELATING

Pattern 1   Pattern 2

A	B	C	D	E
Ruled by Neediness	More Sensitive than Strong	Perfectly Balanced: Both Sensitive and Strong	More Strong than Sensitive	Ruled by Toughness

Only one man in history got it right. He was richly aware of all that he longed for. And that awareness brought with it both pain and hope, both sorrow over what was and joy over what he knew would one day be. He felt his disappointment, but no more keenly than he felt his anticipation. He wept freely over lost relationship and over the cost of recovering it. He was deeply aware of all that went on around him and inside him.

But his sensitivity never led to self-preoccupation or complaint. Rather than merely feeling the hurt of broken relationships in ways deeper than any of us could imagine, he used that hurt to more sharply define and energize his call. He was *delighted* to sacrifice every pleasure—both legitimate joys he had known throughout a past eternity, and illegitimate satisfactions that were his for the taking—for the single purpose of letting people see what his Father was really like. For him nothing mattered more than revealing God as he was and is: an inflexible hater of sin, and a relentless lover of people.

By defining himself in terms of his call rather than by his longings or power, he found the courage to do whatever his call required. He exemplified pure manhood by moving into regions he had never before entered—

compare his preexistence with God before Bethlehem to the darkness of Calvary—and he stayed perfectly on course, never slipping an inch despite tests of unparalleled severity.

He was the only man ever who lived his life exactly at Position C: perfectly sensitive yet unconquerably strong; humbly dependent yet resolutely determined; aware of every nuance in every relationship but unmovably centered in his priority relationship. Jesus blended together virtues in himself that are reliably competitive in us. Sensitivity and strength do not easily coexist. Men with well-developed sensitivities often struggle with feelings of inadequacy, a tendency toward self-pity and complaint, and a nagging sense of discontent. Men more aware of their capacity to move seem to put greater energy into tasks than people. They become hard, distant, and emotionally blunted, protected by a veneer of convincing friendliness.

Men who relate mostly out of their neediness (Position A) are the ones women call weak. Men whose awareness of their needs has made them sensitive to the things that go on inside people (Position B) often fit the manhood criteria laid out by many in the feminist movement: they are gentle, unafraid to cry, and capable of intensely personal discussions. It sometimes takes years before their lack of strength is evident and the damage they do is recognized.

In Positions A and B, neediness compromises relationship. Need-driven men fail to call forth life in another and to enjoy the beauty of another's individuality and independence. Their relationships are often intense but continually troubled, either dying a slow and agonizing death or sputtering along like an old car that spends more time in the shop than on the road.

A tough man's relationships, on the other hand, are more often shallow but stable. But the stability is fragile. Like houses built on sand, a tough man's relationships depend on a conspiracy of pretending that superficiality is satisfying, and that the pleasures of comfort and excitement are acceptable substitutes for the lost joys of communion. When a spouse or friend breaks through the conspiracy and asks the "tough man" for more, the relationship erupts like a long-dormant volcano.

It is then that good things can happen, but they rarely do. Either the erupting partner "repents" and returns to the comforts of shallow stability, or the relationship ends after disintegrating into violent conflict.

Men who are more strong than sensitive (Position D) make up the majority of Christian and secular leadership. Anyone who has been in a leadership position is familiar with the assaults that must be endured. It sometimes seems that personal sensitivities must be dulled in order to survive, and that an attitude of "Just get on with your job" must be cultivated. Nice guys, sensitive men who worry about hurting others and being hurt, finish last. Callous men, whose "tender muscles" have atrophied from chosen disuse, make it to the top and stay there.

Anyone up front must, of course, expect criticism. If I spread my ideas on a public table with the intent of influencing others, my ideas should be studied and critiqued.

But too much criticism directed at leaders reflects an angry spirit of arrogance. Critics who reach spheres of influence on the strength of their criticism of others are often "tougher" men than the leaders they critique. They are insensitive to their impact on people; they roll over any who disagree, with a confidence that appeals to needy men who wish they were tough. They make the difficult life of a leader more difficult.

Most leaders, especially pastors and directors of Christian ministries, feel undervalued and unappreciated. The struggle often feels petty and immature to them, but it doesn't quit. One pastor nearly cried as he told me about the time his elder board questioned if he really needed three weeks vacation.

Sometimes there seems to be no other solution than to build a wall around your heart. The effect in those who manage to build a wall is the loss of rich passion, coupled with the growth of a determination to effectively manage whatever is manageable.

When determination replaces sensitivity, a man becomes hard. He sacrifices the power to move deeply into the life of another. Sometimes his only contact with the world of passion is sex. It's all he can think about. He lives on the brink of moral failure. The solution to his sexual addiction requires more than self-control. It involves a renewed willingness to open his heart to the sting of criticism, a willingness that can feel like laying your head on the chopping block.

If he remains hard-hearted and well-defended against his hurt, he will eventually be ruled more by the need to be tough than by his calling to reflect the character of God. And if the people closest to him do not give him honest feedback about the hurt his growing distance causes in them, then the chances are good he will move farther from the center of the con-

tinuum to the extreme of a man powerfully mastered by his need to be tough (Position E).

And it will seem so necessary, so justified. I have seen pastors writhing in such agony that I almost wished they would numb themselves into toughness in order to survive. But while that would provide short-term relief, it would be a long-term mistake. Tough men destroy relationships; they damage people by requiring them to perform without providing any real nourishment for their souls.

Women in relationship with a tough man often feel

1. *undesired*, because of an unspecified but assumed *ugliness* that "explains" why the tough man never seems to want them
2. *desperate* for someone or something that touches them deeply enough to relieve the pain of loneliness

The victims of tough men are responsible for how they choose to act but not for how badly they hurt. Those victimized are prone to

1. depression: "I have nothing anybody could possibly want. Why bother even trying to relate or to get ahead?"
2. anxiety: "If I can just stay in control of myself, I'll be fine. Oh no! What might happen if I lose control?"
3. addictions: "I cannot stay away from whatever is pleasurable enough to relieve my loneliness, even if it relieves it for just a moment."

Tough men rarely change without first facing their destructive impact on others. That is why it is crucial for folks involved with tough men to risk providing clear feedback about the effect their being ruled by toughness is having on others.[1]

Truly strong men are as different from tough men as maturely sensitive men are from weak men. Tough men share three characteristics that underlie their toughness.

First, *insecurity*. Tough men are driven, by uncertainty about their manhood, to prove themselves. They exhibit their power in order to display what they are not sure they possess. Strong men, on the other hand, feel no need to parade their strength. They have control over their power and unleash it only to further a good purpose.

Second, *shallowness*. Once you get past their competence and charm, men who fall on the tough side of the continuum are not terribly interesting people. They are not especially aware of what is going on inside themselves or others, and feel nothing more deeply than their lust for power. Strong men, however, are not afraid to face all of reality, including ugly things about themselves or others that could provoke overwhelming despair. Strong men remember God and speak with the power of hope into the darkest night.

Third, *misunderstanding*. Tough men have not grasped the essence of true masculinity. They mistake sensitivity for weakness; in their minds, power and strength are the same thing. Strong men know that sensitivity and awareness open the door to mysterious closets that require courage to enter. And their desire to live courageously outweighs their fear of the dark. They define strength as power under control, not power displayed. Tough men fear the closets; they know that their power is no match for the unseen power that inhabits the darkness. They stay out of darkness by never becoming sensitive. And their determination to avoid mystery leaves them even more determined to effectively manage whatever they do face. Their power degenerates into more selfish, more destructive, more malevolent forms of toughness.

All of us fall somewhere on the line, either to the left or right of center. Conscienceless rapists represent an example of the far extreme of power minus sensitivity. Pornography addicts who sacrifice family and respect for one more peep show would be on the other end, living for immediate relief of all the pain that sensitivity without strength produces. Most readers of this book lie somewhere between these two extremes. But none live in the exact center.

Why? Why is it that no man can be held up as a perfect illustration of Position C except one? Why do so few men even come close? Why is modern culture creating reachable standards of manhood that reassure us that we're not doing too badly, and then encourage others to join us in aiming too low?

Men with well-developed sensitivities tend to ask others to come through for them. And when no one does, at least not perfectly, these men become vulnerable to "passive" perversions: pornography, compulsive masturbation, fantasies of women responding to their every wish, dreams of winning the lottery. Men who move boldly but without an awareness of themselves or others sense a different void that makes them attracted to "aggressive" perversions: seduction, sadism, abuse, wealth, and position.

We really are a mess. No one gets it right. Why?

The answer, of course, takes us back to Genesis 3, when Adam refused to speak. A congenital corruption of the design of man has been passed on to every naturally conceived man since. But the fact that our problem is inherited must not be used to let us off the hook of responsibility.

We must face the terrible truth that we are responsible for not speaking with sensitivity and strength, and we must be driven to despair by the even more terrible truth that the urge within us to not speak is too strong to resist on our own. Facing these twin truths will drive us to brokenness, confession, repentance, and trust. Not facing them will leave us with the cherished illusion that things may be bad, but not so bad that God is really necessary.

Something vital is missing in men. We lack the courage and faith to speak into the darkness with life-giving power. And that lack of courage and faith must be understood as sin.

Sin is at the core of our troubles. That is the simple, terrible truth. Nothing "explains" why we sin. The fact that we sin is the foundation for all clear thinking about our troubles. But there is a second level of understanding, a level that builds on the foundation of tracing every trouble back to the Fall. This second level involves a man's relationships with other men.

After original sin, there is no more powerful influence on a man's life than the influence of older men and peers: older men, whose lives we have watched and who have been involved with us, particularly in our formative years; and peers, companions and friends with whom we hang out, swap stories, and tell things that we tell nobody else.

Something truly powerful is available. In Part 3 I suggest that relating as fathers and brothers can help us recapture the lost dream of manhood.

---

1 See *Bold Love,* Dr. Dan Allender and Dr. Tremper Longman, for a thorough discussion of what love demands of people in relationship with someone destructive (Colorado Springs: NavPress, 1992).

Conclusion to Part 2

Not many men enjoy the richness of masculine maturity. Only two of the men who were delivered from Egypt crossed the Jordan River into Canaan. The rest wandered aimlessly in the wilderness until they died.

The path to maturity begins with an honest look at how we relate. What effect do we have on people? If they had the courage, what would our wives, children, and friends tell us about what it is like to be in relationship with us? Do we come across as needy, requiring others to take care of us? Do people feel pressured to handle us well? Or do others experience us as tough, strong to the point that we really don't need much from people, and detached enough that we neither offer nor require intimacy?

Because we lack the courage to move into mystery, we are ruled by either needy passions or tough passions. Neither needy men nor tough men are authentic men.

PART 3

Something Powerful Is Available

A Generation of Mentors

We continue to walk the path to maturity when we admit how deeply we long for a father, *a man who walks ahead of us, letting us know what is possible and calling us to follow, and a* brother, *a peer whose struggles and compassion encourage us to make ourselves known to him as we walk together. When the reality hits us, as it will for most men, that we have neither father nor brother, the overwhelming disappointment can either turn into bitterness or it can drive us to seek God with all our hearts and to become fathers and brothers for other men. For those few who know the joy of being well fathered and richly brothered, the calling is not merely to enjoy these blessings but to provide the same ones for others.*

If men today are willing to look into darkness, to remember God, and then to speak words that bring life to others, if they are willing to walk the steep, narrow, long path toward true masculinity, then perhaps our children will enter their adult years blessed with an older generation of mentors, men who father well as they walk with their brothers toward home.

Chapter 12

Fathers: Men Who Believe in Us

The toughest times came in the early morning, after a useless struggle to fall asleep. He would lie there while his mind took him on a roller coaster ride. There would be a few moments of calm followed by a long, tortured climb up a familiar, steep slope toward dreaded heights, then a sudden drop, a rush of uncontrolled frenzy, and wild, disorganized thoughts plunging him into heart-stopping terror.

The thoughts had one thing in common—they all worried him. The call, from a concerned teacher, about his son's low grades. Why the problem? Was his son lazy? Undisciplined? Rebellious? Was he just slow? What kind of future would he have?

Then there was his daughter. She wasn't pretty. And she had put on weight. At thirteen, appearance mattered more than before. Daddy's hugs and pet names didn't bring the same smile they brought when she was ten.

And then there was his wife. Sound asleep one foot away. But their hearts were miles apart. He wondered why the passion was gone. Nineteen years of ebbing romance left only a hollow shell of commitment. Sometimes a spark returned. But never for long. What would their marriage look like in ten years, when the kids would be gone? Would they ever feel really close again? Would he be able to discard the fantasies and occasional videos that were his only source of sexual excitement?

He looked at the clock—12:23 A.M. His mind kept racing to other worries, without resolving the ones he had already obsessed about. Money. College for his kids. His son might never get in. His daughter needed to—well, her chances of marriage looked slim. He was fed up with careful budgeting, saving twenty dollars a week for a vacation fund, then dipping into it for unexpected expenses. The last time was the plumber's bill. He should have been able to fix the leak himself.

His mind jumped again. Work was boring. A business degree qualified him for middle management and little else. Could he take sitting behind that same desk for another twenty years?

By this time, he knew what he would do. It was a familiar routine. He grabbed his robe and Bible. Then he hurried downstairs before the tears exploded and woke his wife. He sometimes wished they would. It would be nice to be taken care of, to see his wife's concern, to feel her hand on his shoulder. He had felt it before. And it was good, but never enough.

No. Not this time. He would handle it. He would present his worries to the Lord; he would remember God's promises and ask to know his presence. He would find the courage to move with confidence into the confusion of his uncertain and troubling world.

He switched on the light and sat down. He sat in the same chair. Like so many times before, his panic gave way to tears. He sobbed. He dropped to his knees and cried till he could cry no more, wondering if his wife heard. If she did, she didn't come downstairs.

Then he returned to the chair and opened his Bible. He read for a few minutes, then found his mind drifting to thoughts of his father. He lifted his eyes from the page and yielded to the gentle urge directing him toward these thoughts.

The words flashed in his mind, like an announcement on a marquee when the lights go on. The words were these: "Dad's been here!"

He remembered the stories and images: of an illness that cost his dad, who had three kids under ten, his job for two years; of his hard-working mother, who never complained but always looked tired; of his father trying hard to smile but sometimes going for long walks; of the family on their knees together in the bedroom.

He could hear his father's voice: "I'll be working soon, honey. God will provide. Then you'll be able to stay home."

Then the job came. And his dad made good money. Things were better, easier, and happier. But his father still seemed troubled. He could feel the occasional tension between his parents. He never knew what it was. Sometimes their affection seemed forced.

There were more memories of Dad hanging in there: through a few hospital crises; through the normal ups and downs, and the hectic schedules, of his kids; through a five-year stretch of calls from school, knocks on the door from police, and several court appearances; and then through the

pain and embarrassment of his resignation from the church elder board. His older brother had broken his parents' hearts more times than he could count. He remembered his father's tears and his prayers.

The image of Dad praying at mealtime stuck in his mind: the bowed head, the quiet voice with the occasional quiver. "Father, keep us trusting in your goodness. Thank you for your faithfulness through Christ. Make us all followers of him."

The words flashed again: "Dad's been here!" And Dad made it. He wasn't always happy—sometimes he was just plain miserable to be around—but he kept working; he never quit on his responsibilities. And he never stopped caring about his prodigal son.

Now, at age seventy-four, sorrowing beyond words over his wife's recent death after months of suffering, he still wasn't upbeat and chipper. But there was a calmness about him that was more than resignation. He seemed hopeful: not all the time, but when it was there it seemed powerful. He liked to say, "The best is yet to come." Dad was real. His passion for Christ seemed stronger than ever.

When he prayed, the words were the same, but immeasurably richer. The bowed head, the quiet voice with the occasional quiver. "Father, keep us trusting in your goodness. Thank you for your faithfulness through Christ. Make us all followers of him."

He had seen his older son come back to the Lord after two divorces, each occasioned by his son's adultery. And his daughter's youngest child, his only granddaughter, had been through four surgeries in her three years of life. No guarantees for the future.

But his father had walked the path, and he was still walking it after seven decades. Dad had made it.

At two in the morning, he closed his Bible. He hesitated, then self-consciously he bowed his head and, in a quiet voice that slightly quivered, he prayed. "Father, keep us trusting in your goodness. Thank you for your faithfulness through Christ. Make us all followers of him."

He went back to bed and slept. He never woke his wife.

A godly father speaks three messages to his son:

1. "It can be done."
2. "You're not alone."
3. "I believe in you."

Most men in our generation have never received any of these messages from their dads. Something is missing in the souls of unfathered men.

When times get tough, courage is in short supply. The darkness seems too dark to enter. The future looks black. Their fathers' examples give too many men no reason to dream of becoming good men, strong men, virtuous men, loving men. Maybe it can't be done, they think. No one has led the way. No one has demonstrated that it can be done.

Maybe quitting, compromising, indulging in a few moments of cheap pleasure just to relieve the pain, aren't such bad ideas. Perhaps it makes sense to find a wider, more comfortable path than the narrow one we've tried to walk. Who really cares, anyhow? What is there to lose? Suppose we do fall into obvious sin. Lots of folks will shake their heads and say, "Did you hear what happened to Bob? I always did wonder about him. I wonder if he ever really knew the Lord. He sure messed things up. I hear his wife is taking it pretty hard. They'll probably divorce."

No one will care. No one will seek us out and look at us with eyes of hope. And that hurts. It makes our current friendships mean less.

When a father fails his son, he introduces additional battles into his son's life, battles that his son should never have to fight. When a man never hears another man declare, by his life, that pressing on toward maturity is possible no matter what life brings, that he has always been and always will be cared about, and that someone respects his heart and knows that he can make it—a man who never hears these affirmations will experience, in the center of his being, a deep hole that throbs with desperate pain. Something is missing that should be there—and would be there if his father had fathered him well.

This chapter is a call to men to do two things. First, face the reality of your relationship with your father. If it was or is a severe disappointment, admit the loss. Embrace the sorrow. Cry over it. Don't whitewash it with Christian-sounding phrases: "Well, he did the best he could," "I'm thankful that it wasn't worse," "God must have some purpose in all that he allowed." Face up to the hard facts. With all your might, you wish things had been different. You wish they were different now, and you can't think of a way to make them better. It hurts.

Facing things as they are could release the hunger in your heart to know your heavenly Father, but only if the pain doesn't degenerate into a bitterness that just sits there unnoticed and unchallenged. A deepened awareness of your yearnings for a father could make you alert to the men in your life who *have* fathered you: perhaps imperfectly and incompletely but still meaningfully. Your heart might warm to the memory of a grandfather, an uncle, a youth pastor, a high school teacher, a Little League coach. Perhaps you will recognize a spiritual father in Jeremiah or Elijah or Job or Peter, men who struggled, who failed, who felt abandoned and alone, who knew God's faithfulness through trial and chastening—men whose lives tell you it can be done. But face the reality of your relationship with your father. That's the first thing.

Second, develop a vision for what you could mean to other men, particularly to younger men behind you on the path. The void of not having a godly father will not be filled by becoming a godly father to someone else; it may make the pain more acute. But the void will be surrounded by a sense of purpose. And this will bring joy: that unique brand of Christian joy that supports one in one's suffering, rather than ending it; a strange joy that feels more like a reason to go on than like the good feelings of a kid at Christmas.

Young men in college can mentor boys in high school. They can hang out with them, share a pizza, talk about girls, grades, and rules, teach them to play tennis or fix cars or run a computer. Men with their own children have an obvious opportunity and responsibility to convey the threefold message of fatherhood to their offspring. Men without children (both married men and single men), and older fathers who see their adult children only once a year, can all spiritually father other men in their community. This chapter is a call to men to catch a glimpse of what you could mean to those who are watching.

THREE MARKS OF A GODLY FATHER

A godly father is a man who understands what he means to his children, who is humbled by overwhelming joy over the impact he can make for God and terrified by the damage he can do. He is both thrilled and scared. Because of his confidence in God, the thrill is stronger.

He yearns to lead his son, by quiet example and few words, toward godly manhood. As a woman labors to deliver a baby, so this man struggles to bring forth a godly son. In his agony of desire, he is like God, who declares that "like a woman in childbirth, I cry out, I gasp and pant" (Isaiah 42:14) as he anticipates righting every wrong and winning his people to himself.

A godly father is urged on by his highest calling to please his heavenly Father, to become like the Son, and to yield to the Spirit. But the calling to pass on his knowledge of God to the next generation is also strong. As he strives to honor his calling as a father, to remember God, and to speak into darkness in a way that perpetuates the memory, this man does three things that mark him as a godly father.

Mark #1: He walks a good path in sight of his son, to let him know, "It can be done."

There is no sense of display, no posturing intended to impress his son. He simply walks the path God lays out for him, because he trusts God. Even when there is no evidence to support his belief, he clings to what he knows is true about God. He has heard God speak through his Word, and he believes what God has said.

A godly father is a man of faith whose sorrows, though deep and abiding, don't eliminate joy (at least not for long), whose failures are never used to justify hardness, whose struggles, which tempt him to quit, never overcome him. Without knowing it, a godly father's countenance occasionally glows. Not many see it, but a few are dazzled by the brightness of his passion for Christ, a passion that reduces those who watch to awe.

When he learns that his life has deeply encouraged his son to walk the same path, he is surprised—and grateful. He is caught off guard when people speak warmly of his influence. He is so consumed with Christ's glory that he hasn't noticed that a little of it has rubbed off on him.

A godly father doesn't pretend. Life is hard and he knows it. The thorns and thistles prick him, sometimes drawing blood, and the weeds frustrate him. Living outside the Garden is often difficult and occasionally awful. Those who watch him know that he struggles.

He is sometimes more aware of failure than growth. Ask a mature man if he is mature, and he will awkwardly change the subject. When he does reflect on himself, reliably he is amazed that God delights in him and sorrowful that it cost God his Son to make it possible.

A godly father is a storyteller. He teaches, but more through story than lecture. He knows that lessons wrapped up in stories penetrate more deeply and last longer. He tells stories of childhood dreams that gave way to the harsh reality of adulthood.

Listen to a story my father told me in a recent letter:

One memory is extremely vivid. It was my twelfth birthday. I was impressed with the advent of my teens. Thirteen seemed so mature; after all, the next step was twenty. And I had known of some fellows married at twenty.

I sat with Mother on the back porch of an impressive mansion in Chestnut Hill. Aunt Lily was governess there and had permission to have Mother stay there for the summer while the "royalty" were traveling in Europe. I was trying to tell Mother how I would take such care of her when I grew up. We lived at the Baynton Street house then, and I was picturing Mother in the mansion we were then in, with me the provider. As the poet put it: "It was a childish ignorance, but oh what it seemed to be."

Life is very much like that: dreams fade as harsh reality takes over.

That story from my father let me know that he once dreamed dreams, just like I did. Some of his fondest dreams have been dashed, yet he still pursues God and lives faithfully.

Godly fathers tell other stories: of noble dreams that have been realized, of victories as well as defeats, of God's hand on their lives, of those few times when a glimpse of Christ blinded them to all else, of those many times when life seemed just too hard.

As a younger man can see—by listening to these stories—an older man walk the path, the younger man begins to realize that every one of his own struggles has been faced before. He senses a warm hope bathing his weary soul, refreshing him with renewed strength and courage.

"It can be done!" the young man shouts. "He did it. Look at him. He has faced everything I face, he has endured the same fear and heartache and failure, he has asked the same questions and heard the same silence that enrages me. And he still trusts God. He made it. It can be done."[1]

Mark #2: He occasionally turns around and looks at his son to let him know, "You're not alone."

A godly father walks a good path, knowing that his son is walking thirty years behind him. The son watches from behind and, without dialogue with his father, hears the message: it can be done.

Every now and then, with timing that seems frustratingly random and thoroughly unpredictable, a good father stops, turns around, and looks at his son. Until he turns, his son feels the distance between himself and his father: not a cold, barren distance but a distance nonetheless. He longs to hear more from his dad than the message carried by his example, the message that it really is possible to remain faithful to one's calling as a man. He wants to feel connected, heard, taken into account. He yearns to know that the man who cheered at his junior high school wrestling match and stood proudly to applaud at his college graduation is still involved, still interested, still holding his son in his heart. It means the world to an adult son to realize that his father is on his knees before the throne, mentioning his son's name, and to know that his dad feels the pain of every struggle—and the joy of every victory—in his son's life.

When this father turns, his son receives a look that erases all doubt: "Dad still cares. I'm not alone!"

A godly father turns toward his son—perhaps in a letter, a phone call, a visit—not to instruct or admonish. There is a time and place for that sort of communication, but this father's central agenda is to listen. When he turns, he doesn't speak, he invites. Even those letters in which a father can't resist a word of counsel offer advice more than impose it. He respects his son's enormous right and responsibility to make his own choices.

When their eyes meet, even before he speaks the son feels heard. Perhaps his father turned *then*, and not before, because he sensed that his son needed to speak. The Spirit of God often brings a son into the mind of a loving father, who then picks up the phone. I recall—and feel the tears welling up as I do—the evening my father called and said, "I couldn't get you out of my mind last night. I figured God was keeping you there. Anything going on I can pray about?"

A godly father thinks often of his son. Occasionally the thought comes with a force that makes him stop and turn around. And when he turns, he leans toward his son, putting his ear close to his son's mouth as if to say, "I don't want to miss a word you say."

That is exactly what God does with his children who remember him. "The LORD listened and heard" (Malachi 3:16). He listened to a voice that got his attention, and then he bent low to hear. That is the meaning of "listened and heard."

His message in turning is clear: "You're never far from my mind and you're always in my heart. I'm with you. You're not alone!" A godly father gives a taste of the always-listening heavenly Father, the God who collects every tear in a bottle, saving them till the day when he will reveal his good purpose that was in every trial he could have prevented.

A godly father's message is heard by his son: "You're not alone. I'm listening. I hear your pain. I've never told you the details of my battles with lust, greed, and pride, and you've never told me yours. But I know they are there. Nothing would shock me. I too am a man. And nothing puts you beyond the reach of God's love. His grace is as much bigger than our sin as the earth is bigger than one grain of sand. We're both fallen men not yet delivered from the presence of sin. I know life is hard, sometimes terrifying, too often painful beyond words. I ache with you as you worry over money problems, career disappointments, family problems. I feel the weight of your unanswered questions and prayers; I know the darkness you often face. But I know what God has pledged to do. Therefore I can hear about your problems without falling apart or needing to rescue you. In your joys and sorrows, I give you my presence. I am *with* you!"

That's the message of this father's look. In response, the son feels inclined to speak. He doesn't share everything—some secrets are better shared with brothers—but what he does share is heard. Nothing means quite so much to a struggling man than to know that someone who cares is with him, not requiring acknowledgment and appreciation but simply wanting to be there to care and to be available, attentive, and accepting. And as he speaks to his listening father, he finds courage to move farther along the dark path ahead, knowing that his father has already been there and is with him now.

Mark #3: He resumes his walk toward God, trusting God to lead his son to follow, thus saying, "I believe in you."

A godly father does not spend all his time listening to his son. Our Great High Priest can do that, but a human father can't—and shouldn't. If he listens too long and gets too involved in his son's concerns, he will either offer too much help or become discouraged, cynical, or angry. He might send money that would relieve his son of a difficult opportunity for growth, or in frustration give advice that would lead to a power struggle: "You better do what I say, or you'll really mess things up!"

Godly fathers have something more important to do than listen to their sons. For brief seasons, listening may become top priority. But the pattern of a father's life must reflect his commitment to stay on the narrow path, whether his son is following or not.

I remember telling one of my sons, during a difficult period, "You can break my heart, but you cannot destroy my life. I will follow Christ regardless of what you do. My life is hid in Christ. You are important but you are not powerful."

As a godly father resumes his walk and makes that walk his characteristic pattern he puts his son in his proper place. He relieves his son of the unbearable position of being the center of his father's life. The son, freed from a burden he cannot handle and eventually resents, is then more able to cheerfully give to his father that which he possesses and is able to give.

When this father turns away from his son, breaking eye contact to once again fix his eyes on Jesus, his son knows he is not turning away in rejection or indifference. Only the prospect of knowing God better could draw his father away. A godly father knows his son is in good hands, hands more powerful than his, and he learns to rest.

A father who rests means a great deal to his son. Worried fathers convey the expectation that their sons will find some way to mess up their lives. Relaxed fathers communicate that their sons are responsible for their choices before God, a God who will move heaven and earth to win them to obedience.

A godly father's *life* demonstrates the first message: that it's possible, no matter what life brings, to follow Christ. His *presence* assures his son that he is not alone. Someone cares. That's the second message. And his *refusal to hover*—to keep too close an eye on things and to carry his son when his son should find the strength to walk on his own feet—communicates the third message: that he believes in his son. He accepts his son as an individual: responsible for his choices and, by God's grace, capable of making good ones; able to get up after he falls.

> "It can be done."
> "You're not alone."
> "I believe in you."

No man has heard these messages as clearly or consistently as he desires. Godly fathers sometimes fail; they occasionally meddle, depend too much on their sons, or become so preoccupied with their own struggles that they no longer listen well. Often they worry. Their questions convey a lack of confidence in their son's ability to make it.

We must not require perfection from our fathers. Rather we must look for patterns. We must learn to appreciate imperfect but godly fathers who manage to climb back on the good path, who evidence their care genuinely (even if less often than we want), and who know something of resting in the sovereignty of a kind God.

The sad truth, of course, is that most men do not have godly fathers. Very few men can even point to one older man in their lives who has powerfully communicated these three messages. Most have heard three very different messages shouted in their ears:

1. "Life is too hard to live as God requires. A little compromise, some relief that I can count on, some chance to do what makes me feel good about me now, is necessary. A truly godly life? *It can't be done.*"
2. "Sure, I care about you. All right, so I don't listen all that well. C'mon, I got my own problems. Seems to me you should be grateful for all I did when you were a kid. Maybe it's my turn now for a little attention. *I don't really care about you.*"
3. "Look, life isn't getting any easier, you know. Do you have any idea what it's like to grow old? Well, someday you'll find out. I'm doing the best I can. I know it's not so good. *But I doubt if you'll do much better.*"

The thirty-four-year-old son of a wealthy businessman came to his father's deathbed. The last words he heard from his father's mouth were these: "I've left you my company in the will. If I had another son, I'd leave it to him. You're now in charge. My guess is you'll take about a year to destroy everything it took me a lifetime to build."

That son had a hard time finding the courage to go on. He struggled with depression, he spent his money unwisely, and he drank too much. Something vital was missing in his heart, something that his father could have put there.

Was his father to blame for the son's failures? No. His heavenly Father had provided all he needed to live a faithful, responsible life.

But that young man fought battles he should never have had to fight. At the final judgment, perhaps he will receive a greater reward for his lifelong battle against drinking than I will receive for all my teaching and counseling and writing.

Face the reality of your relationship with your father. Face it honestly. Hurt over what is missing. Feel the anger provoked by the pain and neglect. Rejoice in whatever is good. Hear the messages that your father's life has conveyed.

OF ADAM

Then cling to your heavenly Father. Watch his Son perfectly walk a narrow path, and know his life is in you, enabling you to grow in obedience and to never quit. Picture our Great High Priest listening every time we call his name, then bending down to hear every word, every sigh, every scream. Watch him ascend to heaven, with the confidence that his followers will follow, knowing that he will do all that is necessary to keep on drawing us along till we're with him. And look for others—maybe a quiet older man in your church whom you've barely noticed—whose lives tell you that it can be done, that you're not alone, that they believe in you.

Then resolve to become one of those men who quietly speak good messages to the younger men on the path behind them. Count the cost of becoming such a man—it's enormous. But value the privilege and anticipate the joy. There is no higher calling than to represent God to someone by living the life of a spiritual father before them. Become an elder.

---

1   There is a great danger here. Sons often believe they can become no better than their fathers. Every father who has "made it" has in some ways fallen short. Only the Perfect Man *fully* made it. Our calling is to resemble him, not our earthly fathers. And God gives the power to become like Christ even in ways our fathers never realized. Never let a father limit your vision for yourself.

Chapter 13

Brothers: Men Who Share Secrets

It happened so long ago. Why did the memory still dart about the edges of his mind like a germ-ridden mouse skittering around the baseboards of an otherwise clean home?

The temptation was still there. Not all the time, of course; sometimes not at all. But he had that looming sense that at any moment the desire might arise like a monster out of the sea, grab him by the throat, and overpower him.

It started when he was eleven, his first time away at camp. Maybe it was the void created by homesickness that made him so ready.

His buddy—thirteen years old, already muscular, great athlete, camper-of-the-week type of a guy—found it first: a knothole in the wall of one of the girls' cabins. A short walk through the woods, and an easily scaled fence, were the only separation between the boys' and girls' camps.

He had never felt anything like it. Climbing through the window after lights-out, sneaking like a special-unit commando through the woods, crawling noiselessly up to the knothole. And then staring: one eye closed, one eye open—wide open. The girls' counselor let her campers keep their lights on past the appointed hour.

Did those few nights begin the obsession? Why was the desire so strong, the pleasure so compelling and so satisfying that it seemed an irresistible part of his makeup even now, years later?

That same week in camp, he had given his life to Christ. And it was real. His praying parents were thrilled. No one knew what else had begun during those days.

Since then, the battle had been fierce. During his teen years, there were a few movies he should never have seen, ones he still couldn't forget. And there were a few more in his early twenties. Then there was that one late-night visit to the "adult" club.

The movies, he could admit to; even the knothole-peeping seemed more prankish than serious. But two hours in a place like that club. The upscale, friendly people; a mood of everydayness had quieted his conscience until he walked out the door just before midnight.

That was eight years ago, when he was twenty-nine and married, with two little kids, and he and his wife were cosponsors of the church youth group. Now he was thirty-seven, and both of his sons were part of the youth group he still led. The family's wonderful surprise—a baby girl—was now six years old. As chairman of the missions committee, he had led two recent missions trips to eastern Europe; the last trip included the whole family. His life felt like a white shirt with one food stain, which was covered by a carefully positioned tie.

There were times when the idea of abandoning himself to those old, forbidden pleasures seemed to promise something that nothing else could provide, including his faith—no, *especially* his faith. Just the thought of living out his fantasies could relieve a terror within him. It put a lid on the bottomless hole that was always there, waiting with sinister power to one day suck him into its depths. At times, the pleasures of sin seemed his only means of survival, his only hope for joy.

The route from home to work took him within three blocks of that same club. Only a few times in all those years had he gone out of his way to drive by. Once, he slowed down. But never had he even parked his car, let alone got out and gone in.

In his thoughts, he had enjoyed the pleasures available inside that building a thousand times. And he hated himself for it. Every time the memory became a focused image, he felt cheap, soiled, weak—but strangely alive. Even when the memory was dim, it was still there, waiting to capture his mind.

No one knew. A couple of years ago, in his men's group, he had admitted to a problem with lust. Every guy listened supportively, but with the same level of interest that a confession of occasional masturbation might have provoked.

He wanted to tell someone the awful truth in enough detail to make it clear that his sin was big, that indulging it seemed like the gate to paradise.

But who could he tell? His wife? No! He was not sure why, but no. His father? Another clear no. It felt inappropriate.

Two appointed elders at the church stood out as more than managers of ministry. Both were good men. And godly too—but in a conventional sort of way. They seemed more stable than alive. He could imagine their response: sincere concern, promises to pray, but no follow-up, except maybe an occasional "How goes the struggle? I'm still praying for you."

His three closest friends joked too much about sexual things. He resented that. He refused to risk becoming the subject of their irreverent humor.

Stan. The name had never occurred to him before as a potential confidant. He knew him fairly well. They'd had a few lunches together, spent more than a year in the same Bible study group, and shared one evening of long conversation. Stan. Troubled, passionate, struggling, determined, never flippant—funny, but never flippant! The same age, maybe a year younger.

It took him eight months. Finally he did it. He shared his secret with Stan. No lurid detail, but a clear confession of real sin and terror.

Stan listened. A few questions, none that encouraged unnecessary specifics. And not one word or facial expression that conveyed diminished respect. Their conversation felt clean, dignified, important. Stan offered no advice, no attempts to interpret or explain the struggle, no truth reduced to platitude. He spoke more about a vision: for what both their lives could look like in a year—in ten years—as God's Spirit had his way. The vision was not conveyed with a mood of "Hey, relax! You'll be fine!" but more a feeling of "Think what could be. Don't lose heart. It's worth any cost." And he offered to talk more.

That was about a year ago. The struggle had continued. The monster still lurked in the depths. But he felt cleaner, more hopeful, seized by a greater power that called him to something higher.

Once since then, he had driven by the club. He wanted to go in. For a moment, going in seemed like his only hope to feel alive. But now the thought of resisting the urge, of not going in, of shutting down the fantasy of what was in there, seemed important, at times even compelling; to turn away from those pleasures felt like being part of something bigger. Before, saying no to sin seemed like merely obeying a command, something one did to avoid censure, like driving the speed limit when a police car appeared in your rearview mirror.

Stan had called three times in the year since their conversation. Twice he had called Stan. They met together privately only once, for a long Saturday morning breakfast. They talked about Christ, vision, power; only a little about fighting sin. They were still in the same Bible study group. During those evenings when the group met, they laughed together, swapped work stories over refreshments, bantered easily, and sometimes discussed the passage the group had just studied. They mixed naturally with others. Neither felt a pressure to huddle together in a corner.

He found himself becoming a bit more comfortable with the word *victory*. It now contained no hint of complacency, no thought of having matured beyond the terrifying reality of dependence. *Victory* now meant hope, purpose, and movement toward a compelling vision.

He felt more present with his wife during their seasons of conflict. He was more aware that he had something to pass on to his kids, and was more eager to do so. He was more hungry for God and passionate about life. Sexual temptations, though still strong, felt less threatening than the black hole that could still pull him into its meaningless depths. And the terror of the black hole felt, at times, less powerful than his hunger to know Christ.

Whenever he heard someone say the word *brother*, Stan always came to mind.

Fathers encourage by leading the way, by walking *ahead* of us on the path. Brothers encourage by sharing our struggles, by walking *with* us.

In an informal study of four thousand men, one man in ten reported that there was, in his life, someone he looked to as a father. Only a handful of men know the encouragement of another man whose life proclaims, "It can be done. You're not alone. I believe in you."

That same survey indicated that one in four had a brother: not merely another male offspring of the same parents but a peer with whom they felt no shame.

If that survey is accurate, then ninety men out of every one hundred are unfathered, men without a mentor. Seventy-five of that same one hundred have no brother. They are men who live with secrets.

Secrets come in several varieties. There are secrets involving *specific events*, memories of things others have done to us, or things we have done. There are secret *internal realities*: urges, interests, struggles, motives, thoughts, beliefs, or feelings that we regard as unacceptable, that we think would spoil any relationship in which they were known. Sometimes the things we hide are *vague but powerful impressions*, usually involving an unnamed but terrifying sense of our own despicableness, a sense that—we fear—others would confirm if given the chance.

Secrets have three major effects:

1. They weaken *courage*.
2. They isolate their keepers from *community*.
3. They erode a legitimate sense of personal *confidence*.

To understand the lethal damage created by these effects, recall the three-part definition of manhood:

Men are called to

1. look deeply into mystery, to honestly face the unresolvable confusion of life
2. remember the character and deeds of God, to see the unseen story of God revealed in Scripture and in the events of our lives
3. move into the chaos of life, with the power to restore order and release beauty

The three effects of keeping secrets will present substantial obstacles to men who long to honor their three-part calling. Let me explain.

Effect 1: Secrets weaken courage, making it less likely that men will look deeply into mystery.

Every man questions whether he has what it takes to survive the challenge of looking honestly at life. Men with secrets are convinced they don't.

In conversations with themselves—which they sometimes don't consciously hear—men with secrets wonder, "How could a man like me handle the real challenges of life? How could I enter the messiness of relationships and hang in there with the power to do good, when I know what I'm really like? My only hope is to stay so far away from what I can't handle that I am never exposed as the inadequate man I am. The best I can do is find something I can do well, and put all my energies there."

Men who keep secrets are terrified at the prospect of exposure. But something else terrifies them more. The lesser fear—exposure of something they know but no one else knows—sometimes protects them from having to face the greater fear. Like a man so preoccupied with his sprained ankle that he doesn't notice the pain in his chest, men may focus attention on what they are hiding to keep them from facing something far worse.

When a man shares his secrets, his first reaction is often relief. But soon he becomes aware of a deeper fear. Men without secrets see more clearly the terrifying nature of existence, its profound uncontrollability, and its power to destroy every dream. When we get beyond our tightly held secrets, they seem petty in light of what we then begin to face. We slowly (sometimes over years) become aware of a yawning black hole that threatens to swallow us into its depths. The everyday pressures of life—unpaid bills, rebellious kids, relational conflicts—feel like only the tip of an iceberg. Something more is lurking beneath, a sinister force that is arranging for our lives to crumble around us and leave us in misery, alone, with no hope of escape.

Keeping secrets is cowardly. It helps us stay away from the far more significant challenge that faces every man, which is to stare into the darkness of a life that makes no sense and, in that darkness, to move with joy. Men who keep secrets never find the courage to look at the mystery of life. They fall short of the first element of the call to manhood.

Effect 2: Secrets encourage isolation, making it difficult to see the hand of God in community, and therefore giving men less to remember.

Isolation is perhaps the most obvious effect of keeping secrets. We feel alone, disconnected, shut out, like strangers in a crowd in which we want to belong. Secrets create distance.

When I was a teenager, I developed a case of severe acne on my chest. For more than a year, I kept medicated gauze on an open wound shaped like a rectangle, perhaps four by six inches in size. No one outside my family (except the doctor who was treating me) knew the secret that I kept hidden beneath my shirt. Before and after gym class, I changed quickly, facing the wall while I buttoned my shirt. I never showered at school.

I did whatever was required to keep my secret. And that task was far more meaningful to me than engaging in social opportunities. In every crowd, I was aware that I was hiding something that—if discovered—would set me apart as unusual, disfigured, hard to enjoy. I never relaxed enough to engage in community with the ease and naturalness I longed to experience.

Something similar happens to every man who keeps secrets, who lives to avoid exposure of that which he fears would mark him as an outsider. What he dreads comes upon him. He finds himself alone, isolated from the community he was designed to enter.

And it happens not only in community with people. It happens in relationship with God.

Grace makes it possible to stand unashamed in the presence of God. It restores the dream of belonging where one most wishes to belong. But men who keep secrets never realize that opportunity. Whatever their external posture might be, their inner man is always looking down, away from the possibility of contact with anyone's eyes, especially God's.

The effect is serious. Not only do secret-keepers feel that some part of them remains disengaged during routine conversations, but when the topic turns to spiritual things, these men feel more like eavesdroppers than participants, like the kid pressing his face against the window of a closed candy store. They find little comfort in thoughts about God. Neither prayer nor Bible study connects with the hunger within them.

Forgetting God becomes a way of life, as natural and as necessary as breathing. Remembering God, thinking about him, speaking with others about him, feels stiff and forced. Sexual thoughts, or discussions about the last football game, connect far more powerfully with something deep inside. And keeping God out of our minds makes it easier to enjoy our secret sins.

Men with secrets do not remember God the way he wants to be remembered. They therefore fail to keep the memory alive or to pass it on to others. They fall short of the second part of their calling to be men.

Effect 3: Secrets erode confidence, robbing men of the joyful anticipation of moving with power to restore order and to release beauty in the community around them.

This third effect of keeping secrets makes it difficult for men to even imagine themselves moving powerfully into another person's life.

Among its unparalleled virtues, the gospel will "cleanse our consciences from acts that lead to death" (Hebrews 9:14). It has the power to silence our accusers, to close the mouth of the one who delights to remind us of failures we would most like to forget. A troubled conscience shouts a destructive message that makes it difficult to hear the Spirit whisper his life-giving message: "You belong to Christ. So completely are your sins forgiven that the Father cannot remember them. I have taken up residence within you to empower you to become like the Son and to advance the Father's purposes. Rejoice. You have reason to sing."

Secret-keepers hear a very different message, which they sometimes think is coming from the Spirit: "You're still a mess. You should be much farther along by now. I'm just about disgusted enough to give up on you. The only evidence of creativity in your life is your ability to figure out new ways to fail."

With that message ringing in their ears, these men refuse to move anywhere without a code, without some easily followed plan that promises success. They stubbornly retreat into the sphere of management, determined to stay away from mystery, confident only that they lack the wisdom to handle the rich challenges of life.

Men with secrets do not move into the mystery of relationships. They see no point in it. It would only lead to failure. They therefore fall short of the third element of the call to men.

SHARING SECRETS WITH A BROTHER

Men with secrets cannot live out their calling. No man should live in the isolation of embarrassment. The Bible is clear: we are to confess our sins to each other. That instruction is followed by the reminder that "the prayer of a righteous man is powerful and effective" (James 5:16).

Notice that James says a righteous *man*, not righteous *men*. Perhaps he is encouraging us to confess our faults to individuals, not necessarily to groups. Whether or not that is implied in this passage, most would agree that indiscriminate openness is not a good thing. But it *is* a good thing to find one man with whom you can be fully open, someone with whom you can walk side by side on the journey home, with no secrets between you.

There are, of course, no secrets with God. "Nothing in all creation is hidden from God's sight. Everything is uncovered and laid bare before the eyes of him to whom we must give account" (Hebrews 4:13). And we are invited, even with every secret fully exposed to God, to approach him "with confidence, so that we may receive mercy and find grace to help us in our time of need" (Hebrews 4:16).

And the fact that God's grace frees him to accept us, even though in ourselves we are unacceptable, should affect the way we relate in Christian community. The body of Christ must faithfully reflect the character of Christ.

Something happens within a man when he makes known to another man that which is least attractive about himself. When we share our secrets with a brother, something happens that will happen in no other way. Pouring our hearts out before God is foundational. But presenting ourselves as we really are, with every secret laid bare, to one other human being puts us in touch with the liberating power of God's grace in a manner that no secret-keeper will ever know.

When a man takes another man into his confidence, when two men walk together and agree that only unconfessed sin and tightly held secrets can put us beyond the reach of sanctifying grace, three life-giving messages are heard:

1. "Nothing you are or have ever done dooms you to defeat. God's arm is long enough to reach into the deepest black hole, and strong enough to lift you out. We will walk together, with a courage to face life honestly that nothing can take from us. *Together we will look into the dark, terrifying confusion of life.*"

2. "You have something powerful to give. Your secrets do not define you. Beneath your worst failure and deepest wound lies a man, a bearer of God's image, who can know God and reveal him only in community. With hope and joy, you can look up into the face of God. You can remember him and pass the memory along until the memory yields to the dazzling reality of his presence. You have something to say. So do I. *Together we will seek to know God and to realize the vision he has for our lives.*"

3. "There is a calling on your life that no secret can remove. God has made the mystifying choice to work through redeemed failures. And we continue to fail; but we are men with an appetite for God, an appetite that keeps us moving into the darkness, where he can be most fully known and most fully revealed. We are men called by God to restore the order of his design and to release the beauty of his character until the day when he will stun us all with the order of a new world and with the beauty of Christ revealed in his children. *Until then, together we will speak into the dark reality of this world, on his behalf.*"

We must prayerfully seek a man to be our brother. But even more, we must prayerfully seek to be a brother for another man.

There is an untapped reservoir of power in Christian community. Some of that power will only be released when men become brothers.

Chapter 14

The Dream Restored: A Generation of Mentors

Optimism in a fallen world is generally misguided. Although gloominess is not the right antidote, it still must be said that folks with a reliably cheerful outlook are often naïve. And their naïveté may have about it a stubborn quality that can feel more like a choice than an accident of temperament.

In Christian circles, optimism typically is built on the idea that God's central purpose is to bless us with the kind of life we want or to transform culture into a friendlier environment for Christians. Counselors specialize in solving our problems and relieving our pain. Christian leaders tell us that our prayers, activism, and united influence will turn our nation around and usher in a godly society. Both groups may be guilty of distracting us from the real call of God.

It is our individual lives and our Christian communities that must turn around. We must learn to continue serving Christ when problems come and to draw closer to Christ in the middle of unrelieved suffering. Whatever influence we have on culture must be the product of a deep passion for God, a passion that makes us into attractively different people and keeps us struggling together in a community that is imperfectly but genuinely loving.

Social crusading is so much easier than finding God. Fighting for Christian standards sometimes seems to involve a belligerence that compromises humility, or an aggression that masquerades as courage. And working to overcome our personal problems requires less of us than seeking God with all our hearts. Neither social crusading nor solving our problems stirs the kind of self-awareness that lets us know that the real problem is within ourselves.

Becoming godly people is no simple matter, unless you define godliness as merely avoiding obvious sin (and getting others to do the same) or as resolving our problems so that pleasant feelings return—feelings that we can then call victory.

But when godliness is understood to involve a passion for God that continually transforms the way we relate to others, it makes us willing to postpone personal comfort till a later day. This godliness stirs a desire to know Christ that is stronger than every other desire, and it shows us that our greatest enemy is ourselves. Becoming like Christ becomes our consuming ambition.

The great need of our day will not be met by training more counselors. It will not be met by leaders calling us to join the fight against moral pollution in our society.

The greatest need in our world today is simply this: godly men and women who possess and display a quality of life that reflects the character of God, and that provokes curiosity in others about how they too can know God well.

If we can recognize the path to spiritual maturity, if we can identify and respond to the appetite for Christ placed within us by God's Spirit, then perhaps thirty years from now my dream for a generation of mentors might come true. Think of it! Spiritual fathers and mothers, godly brothers and sisters, creating communities of people who care about outsiders and draw those outside the circle into something they've never known but have always wanted. Communities of people whose passion for Christ is stronger than their grudges, their competition for recognition, and their jealous feelings. Christians who have been mentored for long seasons of time by spiritual fathers and mothers, and who—as a result—are so consumed with knowing Christ better that they hang in there through the messiness of community and never give up on themselves or others, because they know that Christ hasn't given up—and never will. They have seen him in their mentors.

What would the church look like if men began to speak? If we were broken by the sinfulness of our unmanly patterns of relating and were willing to give up our status as experts and pay the cost of becoming elders? What would happen in our church communities if men in leadership went beyond their natural strength—their ability to manage ministries—and in dependence on God led their congregations toward an inspiring vision?

What movement of the Spirit might occur if, in every church, a few men passionate for God drew others to relentlessly pursue God? What would happen if many of these men then related to one another with an openness that led to struggling onward together?

What would be the impact on families if men courageously faced the terrifying confusion in the world, and then remembered enough of God to powerfully and wisely move into their relationships?

What would take place in the hearts of women if men had a vision for their wives, daughters, sisters, mothers, and female friends, a vision they pursued with a gentle strength, and a poetic passion, that no woman had the power to stop?

Our culture is caught up with everything but finding God. It is more beneficial to use Christ than to know him. We use him to make ourselves feel better, to develop a plan for making life work, to keep hoping that we'll get everything we think we need to be happy. We rarely worship him.

An eighty-four-year-old man wanted to speak with me after I preached at a Bible conference. I saw him waiting while I chatted with a group that had gathered. When the folks left, I quickly made my way over to this short, elderly man. He put both hands on my shoulders and told me a story: "Dr. Crabb, I am eighty-four years old. Five years ago my wife died after fifty-one years of a good marriage. I cannot express the pain that I feel every morning as I drink my coffee at the kitchen table alone. I have begged God to relieve the terrible loneliness that I feel. He has not answered my prayer. The ache in my heart has not gone away. But . . ." and here the gentleman paused and looked past me as he continued ". . . God has given me something far better than relief of my pain. Dr. Crabb, he has given me a glimpse of CHRIST. And it's worth it all. Whenever you preach, make much of Christ!" He turned and walked away.

How sad that we spend our energy fixing problems, boosting self-esteem, recovering from shame, overcoming anger, and finding ways to be delivered from spiritual bondage. None of these things are wrong in themselves, but they must be the outgrowth of a fascination with Christ. A fascination with Christ changes the way we do everything else.

No longer do we need to look for formulas when we're confused, or "supernatural distractions" when we're bored. No longer must we require guarantees to relieve the terror of uncertainty, or stay busy so that we never have to be alone with ourselves. No longer do we have to ask something from life that it cannot give.

Disillusionment with the church, discouragement with our lives, and disappointment in others are all the product of the core disease of Western culture: we demand the satisfaction of a life that is working well. Suffering is something to relieve. Problems are things to be fixed. Distressing emotions must be replaced with pleasant ones.

People who persuade us that they know how to relieve suffering, fix problems, and change unwanted emotions become our leaders, experts who get our attention, because they tell us that our dreams for a better life can be realized. (See Jeremiah 29:8.) In these last days filled with self-lovers who treat self-hatred as the greatest sin, we have gathered a great many teachers around us, teachers who tell us what our itching ears want to hear (2 Timothy 4:3).

Our culture is moving in a wrong direction. We are in a determined, frantic flight from God. Pascal once wrote:

> When everything is moving at once, nothing appears to be moving, as on board ship. When everyone is moving toward depravity, no one seems to be moving, but if someone stops, he shows up the others who are rushing on, by acting as a fixed point.[1]

To resist the wrong movement of culture by standing still is the beginning of good movement. To expose movement away from God by remaining still enough to hear him tell his story is the calling of an elder, a mentor, a spiritual father, a man who then moves toward God and others.

Perhaps a second reformation will build on the foundation of the first one by calling us to know the Person who is our justification. Perhaps it will come through a shift from depending on experts who know principles for effective living to pondering the wisdom of elders who know Christ. It is my hope that in our churches, God will do a fresh work—quiet but deep—that will lead men to know God well enough to father those following behind, and to brother those walking side by side on the path toward true maturity.

The call to authentic manhood will never be popular. It is a call to loneliness, to giving without appreciation, to suffering as the necessary means for learning wisdom. It is a call to accept—without complaint or fear—that the most important parts of life are confusing, a call to turn off the artificial light supplied by experts and move into the darkness of God's light.[2] It is a call to weariness so profound that the exhortation to continue well-doing seems cruel.

Men who respond to this call, who set their sights on becoming fathers and brothers, must be willing to pay a price so enormous that only a clear glimpse of Christ will keep them going. The price first includes a willingness to fight lifelong battles: battles against lust, where victory must be defined as resisting—not always reducing—powerful urges; battles against friction in relationships that sometimes cannot be understood, and occasionally will end in the heartbreak of rupture; battles against discouragement so heavy that it will threaten to stop all good movement.

Second, the call to manhood requires a willingness to cling to what God has said, during long seasons when there is no evidence to visibly demonstrate its truth.

And third, the price of following the call involves a willingness to be reduced to a level of humility at which we are capable of no movement toward others, a level at which the only thing we can do is to allow others to pray for us.

The path to manhood is difficult—but worth every step. It provides meaning that is available nowhere else. There are seasons of contentment and moments of joy that bring us higher than fallen men ever imagine they could rise. At times we can neither predict nor control, the Spirit of God pulls back the curtain and fills our eyes with a vision of Christ that enables us to say with Paul, "Our light and momentary troubles are achieving for us an eternal glory that far outweighs them all" (2 Corinthians 4:17).

The concepts presented in this book may seem abstract. To men who demand a code, they will necessarily be frustrating. But to the many men who long for a richer experience of their manhood, we hope these concepts will guide that longing toward its realization.

In an effort to put a little more flesh on the skeleton, we close our book by continuing the personal stories each author began at the front of the book. We briefly share something of our continuing journeys toward the type of manhood we have described. As you read these concluding chapters, may your desire to know Christ deepen until it exceeds every other passion. And may you move along the path to becoming fathers and brothers, spiritual men who develop into a generation of mentors.

1   Quoted in *Christianity for Modern Pagans,* by Peter Kreeft (San Francisco: Ignatius Press, 1993), 95.

2   "The darkness of God's light" is an intriguing phrase attributed to Oswald Chambers, drawn perhaps from Isaiah 50:10–11.

THE STORY CONTINUES

AL ANDREWS

I had been taking piano lessons for seven years before I began taking them from Mr. Buelow. My other teachers had been proficient in teaching me the basics, and while he emphasized them as well, he was interested in something more. One day, at the conclusion of a lesson, he asked me to memorize a small music book containing seven or eight short pieces. When I returned several weeks later, having committed them to memory, I played the pieces for him.

After I finished, he commented that technically I was accurate in what I played. I had performed the pieces as they had been written. Yet according to him, there was something missing.

"You did not play the music with feeling," he said. "Play the pieces the way you think the composer meant for them to be played." To a thirteen-year-old, such statements could easily be discounted as the weirdness of an adult, or the eccentricities of a music teacher; but the firmness in his voice convinced me to make another attempt.

Not long into the second attempt, he stopped me. "That's not it! Try it again." Another try. Another directive to stop—this one with more emphasis. "Play the piece with your heart. Play it with passion!" Frustrated but more determined, I sat for a moment, looking at the keyboard as if begging the keys for an answer as to how to play. I thought for a moment, placed my fingers on the keys, leaned into the piano, and played.

As long as I live, I'll never forget that moment. A different music came out of the piano. A different passion was released from me. "That's it!" he said. "That's it! You've got it!" Finally I understood him. This time, I knew what he meant. I played on. Exuberantly I continued to play, reveling in his enjoyment—but far more in my own passion and freedom.

It was a wonderful day. A day when something deep inside me was released, and the result was music: the rich and passionate music of the soul.

A few weeks later I quit.

The day I quit has haunted me for years. As I've watched others play the piano, I've wished it could be me. I have regretted the decision. But at the time, quitting seemed the only possible route.

To what? Why would I quit? Why—after experiencing something both rich and powerful—would I stop? Why would I ensure that a passionate moment wouldn't be repeated? When a good and talented mentor pushed me beyond my known realms to reach for greater heights, why would I retreat? As I've thought about possible answers to these questions, I've discovered that three are central to how I've lived my life.

The first is obvious: I was afraid. Did I fear failure? In part. But more likely, I was afraid of losing control. Even at a young age, I had worked hard at making my life as orderly and predictable as possible. I didn't get into arguments, nor did I engage in anything with too much passion. I wanted to live without too many highs or too many lows, always knowing what to expect. Though I might not accomplish many great successes, I wouldn't experience much failure either.

Playing music that was not on the page might lead me to an unexplored realm, a more dangerous and risky place. I wanted to live my life on the music book page: the notes are there, the instructions are there, the beginning and the end are known. When I moved beyond the predictable and into something more chaotic, there was a greater chance that my incompetence would be exposed. I would be more likely to make a fool of myself; there would be a greater possibility of failure. Like most men, I do not enjoy such exposure. It is better to follow the notes, play by the rules, and get through unscathed. Avoid risk. Stay away from chaos.

The second reason I quit is a little more subtle. If I did well, more would be required of me. I had visions of more difficult pieces, more recitals, more work, more expectations. It was a weight and pressure I didn't want and certainly didn't need. If I remained mediocre, I wouldn't have to worry about it. I wouldn't stand out.

The third reason I quit is not at all obvious but very real. I hated my passion. I knew it would usher unpleasant things into my life. What is true of the piano player is also true of the disciple, the lover, the athlete, the artist, the writer. If he does well, he will suffer. This suffering will be experienced in both persecution and loneliness. If a man stands out for his passion, though some will like him, many will hate him. Jealousy and envy are unleashed in the presence of excellence. But more importantly, a man's deep passions touch on something of heaven, a taste of what will be one day. With that taste comes the loneliness of being a pilgrim who's not yet home but who yearns for it. As he yearns, he feels an unquenchable hunger that will not be satisfied in this life.

It hurts to live with hunger. It's painful to be homesick. If I live without passion, doing a job that is merely good enough to get by, then I'll not feel the hurt and I'll not suffer.

Did I know all of this when I stopped taking piano lessons? Of course not. At the time, my excuse was that I wanted to play trumpet in the high school band. It has only been in thinking back that I've seen my departure as not a movement toward another instrument but rather a flight from something else. Whatever I felt that afternoon was too dangerous. The discomfort of it overshadowed the exhilaration. It was too much, and my fear left me feeling hollow.

For much of my life, I've felt that empty place inside. Something was missing in me. It was as if I were built on some cosmic assembly line, and someone forget to put in a critical part. I have looked diligently to find it. I've searched for it in seminars, listening carefully for the word or phrase that would make me complete. I've studied book after book, hoping for some gem of wisdom to leap from the page. I've used passionate, talented friends, attempting to get something from them that I thought I didn't have, hoping to absorb into myself whatever they could give. But my search has been futile. The missing part has remained a mystery.

As I've spoken with other men about my search, most recognize my quest as their own. "I know what you're talking about," they say, with a hint of relief in their voices. "I thought I was the only one." Though their stories are different, they each talk eloquently about something that is missing inside them. The search for the missing piece is varied, and what they find to fill themselves works only for a time. Eventually it fails.

My story reflects a reality that is present in every man. There is something inside all of us that yearns to be expressed. It is both passionate and creative. It doesn't need to be learned. It doesn't need to be created; it already has been. It is there, built into men at birth, waiting for release. And when it is released, it is terrifying. I know that now, but for many years, I did not.

On occasion, I knew that there was something within me that was rarely seen. It peeked out when I felt strongly about something, when I stood up for what I believed, when I accomplished a difficult task, when I tackled a difficult situation and got through it. But because it was so rare, the occasional burst was more frustrating than encouraging. It only proved my sense of futility. It wasn't until my mid-thirties that I experienced something more.

In the summer of 1989, I stepped off a plane in Nashville, Tennessee, to meet Nita Baugh. This was only the second blind date of my life. The first one, in college, was a disaster. Though I had vowed "Never again!" the prodding of a trusted friend and matchmaker convinced me to give it another try.

From the moment we met at the airport, both of us knew that something was different. It wasn't love at first sight, but we both recognized an instant connection. During the weekend that followed, we sailed on a windblown lake, enjoyed long talks over coffee, dined at a romantic Italian restaurant, and were engrossed with each other's company. I was captivated with this woman. As hard as I tried, I couldn't find something wrong with her, something that would give me an excuse to run away. One evening during that first visit (which lasted several days), I awoke suddenly in the middle of the night. My heart was racing and I was covered in sweat. With the panic came a familiar feeling of dread. "I'm making a big mistake," I thought. "What if she's not the right one? I need to get out of here." I'd had these kinds of thoughts before, and eventually felt this panic in every other relationship I'd had with a woman. Each time, the feelings led to my withdrawal. I had assumed that they were an indication that something was wrong with the relationship. They were warning signs to be heeded. But the feelings had never appeared only two days into a relationship. This was too soon! If I'd had access to a car that night, I might have tried to escape to the airport. Without one, I decided instead to pray.

I asked God to remove the anxiety. He didn't. I asked him to give me a sign. He remained silent. The panic continued into the night. It was an anguishing and frightening time. After a time of waiting and wrestling, something very new came out of me. "These feelings are inaccurate!" I yelled. "I'm thirty-four years old, and sick of running from women. I'm lonely, because my panic always wins. I like her, and I'm not leaving this time!" I was in a battle and I knew it. I also knew that the fight I was having was bigger than this relationship. It involved something more. It involved my stubbornness, my fear to move, my lack of willingness to take a risk, my tendency to flee from passion.

My panic, though significant and strong, was never my final reality. The fears were a convenient excuse I used in order to keep from moving. I was attracted to Nita, and I had enjoyed the weekend. I was intrigued with her and wanted to pursue her. I didn't want to retreat because of an unexplained fear that was more useful than true. That night I prayed a different prayer. I confessed my own cowardice and the harm I had done to others because of it. I prayed that I would fight well against my desire to retreat, and that I would love. I went to sleep, awaking the next morning with a new commitment. Six months later Nita and I were engaged, and in a year we were married. The panic never came back. That surprised me.

In this story, I am not offering a guideline for fearful men to follow. I am not saying that one certain prayer will end all fear. Many have prayed similar prayers and have spoken strong words of intention, only to find themselves more anxious than ever.

I don't really know why my anxiety left me. But I do know that I made a choice that was different, a marked change from previous directions. The choice was to move in spite of fear, proceeding into the chaotic, thrilling, risky darkness of relationships. It involved the belief that there really was something more in me to be released. The results have not always been glorious. There are times when I still retreat to old ways, when I fail to move and instead fall back into weak and predictable patterns. But there has been a change.

Two images have guided my life: the Little Leaguer who was afraid to swing and the piano player who quit when he felt passion. They are images that reflect both the usefulness of fear and the reassurance of the choice to play things safe. I have lived with the results that this choice produces: feelings of incompetence, loneliness, and insecurity. Had there been no change, I would have lived my life as a defeated man. But there has been a shift and a desire for something more.

What's made the difference? What has moved me to get moving? It has not been a response to an inspirational challenge, nor has it been a response to an astute insight about manhood. It has been the realization that I was a man who had gone to a far-off place.

I am a prodigal son. But my journey was not to a foreign land to spend my inheritance on the wild life of strong drink and seductive women. I lived far more acceptably. My travels took me to a land of safety, where I served the gods of predictability and passionlessness. For a time, I enjoyed that life; but then pangs of hunger began to break through the apparent security of the life I had chosen. Like the prodigal in the Bible, the thing that brought me home was hunger: the hunger of a man. I wanted to reflect the image of the Father, to be deeply invested, deeply passionate, and wildly unpredictable. My return involved the confession that I had chosen another path, that I was sorry for the harm I had caused, and that I longed to be home with my Father. Becoming a man requires me to come home again and again.

Several months ago, on my fortieth birthday, my wife surprised me with the gift of a piano. And she gave me a copy of the sheet music I was playing years ago when I quit. When the piano arrived at our home, I sat on the bench and looked at the new, white, glistening keys. Nita and our seven-month-old son, Hunter, sat beside me as I began to play. This time, I experienced it, enjoyed it, and knew that I wouldn't run. With tears, Nita too enjoyed the music, knowing all that it represented. Hunter, intrigued with these strange new sounds, smiled his bright, toothless grin.

I love my family. I love people. And I love Christ. I therefore don't want to run. I would rather move with courage in order to tell—through my life—the story of redemption. I know I will stumble, and I know I will again go away to foreign lands for a time. But now I know that the passionate music and the sumptuous banquet in the Father's house will beckon me home every time, until I'm there to stay.

DON HUDSON

*If people bring so much courage to this world the
world has to kill them to break them, so of course it kills
them. The world breaks everyone, and afterward many are
strong in the broken places.*

Ernest Hemingway, *A Farewell to Arms*

He was the little boy I never wanted.

Perhaps I should explain. It's not that I despise children. Nor do I find
them intrusive. On the contrary: for most of my life, I dreamed of having
children. The problem was that as much as I wanted to be married and have
children, I didn't think it was possible for *me*. How could I be a father, when
I did not grow up with my father?

Growing up, I always saw myself as inadequate and defective—as broken. And now, having a child would only be a minute-by-minute reminder
of my deficiencies. How could I possibly give something to a child if I had
nothing to give in the first place?

Our son was given to us in spite of my self-doubt. He was born four
and a half years into our marriage, and we named him Donald Michael Martin Hudson. We named him to carry the names of his father and grandfathers. If you recall my story, you'll remember that I changed my name at
the age of six. Names are important to me. I named myself because I wanted
an identity during an empty and disconnected time in my life. And now I
named my son after his fathers so he will know that he is connected to good
men—so he will know that he is not alone. I want him to remember the
men who love him.

There are sacred moments that change us forever, moments that send
us on a journey we could never imagine. My son's birth was one of these
moments for me. I was smitten by him. I was beside myself over this little,
wrinkly, lizardlike creature. The dam in my heart burst on the day of his
birth, and I was flooded with love for my son.

Yet that same flood brought more than love. It also brought a new worry, one I had never encountered: what if I lose this little boy? Suddenly two strong emotions raged inside me: overwhelming love and paralyzing fear. I wanted to run to him, and yet, I wanted to run away from him.

Then and there I understood that I had made a serious error. My love for this little boy had captured me. I had always kept a safe distance from everyone. Then if anyone rejected me, I would not hurt, because I was close to no one. Yet in the labor room that day, I stood helpless as a tiny boy stole my heart. He blew into my world like a raging western storm and knocked the fragile strands of my emotional cocoon away.

One month later one of our worst nightmares came to pass. On the Fourth of July weekend, my wife and I wanted to get away for a few hours. We had planned to attend a concert with some good friends. But when Friday afternoon came, Suzanne felt uncomfortable about going to the concert. "I just don't feel good about leaving," was all she could explain. I had learned by then to trust her intuition. We decided I would go to the concert, since I was the one who most enjoyed the band.

Late that night when I returned, I instinctively knew something was terribly wrong. I walked into the house, and as I approached our bedroom, I could hear Michael screaming in pain. My wife had a terrified look on her face.

"What's wrong?" I asked. I took Michael into my arms and tried to comfort him. "He feels hot. Have you taken his temperature?" In her panic and frustration, she had forgotten to take his temperature.

It was high, very high. We knew enough about infants to know we had to get Michael to the hospital immediately. When we arrived, the nurse took his temperature. The emergency room exploded into life. A nurse rushed to call a pediatrician. The doctor arrived within minutes and immediately explained that our son was in serious danger. Michael could have spinal meningitis. The doctor ordered a battery of tests.

I was dazed by all the terror and commotion. I had no idea what spinal meningitis meant, but my mind raced with thoughts of brain damage or death. The doctor asked us to stay in the waiting room while his team ran the tests, but I refused. I could not bear to leave Michael alone.

I was slowly crumbling inside. I had gone through many medical emergencies of my own, but I had never been this terrified. And this time was different. This crisis was not about me; it was about my son. There wasn't much time for thinking.

An X-ray technician burst through the door and ushered Michael and me into a room to take an X ray of his lungs. The next moments are burned in my memory. The technician disappeared, and I turned my thoughts to God. I was riddled with fear—but I was furious! How dare God toy with my son! Holding Michael close to my chest, I paced the room and I battled with God. Within moments though, my anger subsided, and I began to pray a strange prayer: "Father, please don't take him—take me. If this is serious, and you are going to take him, please take me instead. Let him live."

As absurd as my prayer was, I meant business. I don't suggest this prayer as a model for facing adversity, but at that time, it was something I could not force down. It was a prayer I had to pray.

Fortunately, instead of spinal meningitis, our son had a serious viral infection. It passed within three days. During those hours of crisis, however, a sacred moment had broken in upon me: I learned that I was ready to lay my life down for my son. I approached a fleeting glance of what it means to live *for* another. Later that week, I found myself reflecting in wonder: "I think I'm beginning to get the point. My life is not my own. I am called to live for others. And I *want* to. Maybe that's what it means to be a man."

On that night, I would not have hesitated one second to give my life in order to spare my son's. Waves of fatherhood had arisen from within me and demanded that I act for Michael. I could not control it, and I could not refute it.

The possibility of losing my son taught me surprising truths about being a man. I learned that I already have what it takes to be a man—that there are passions deep within me. There are strong emotions and beliefs raging inside. No one talked me into saying that prayer for my son. In fact, the intensity of my feelings stunned me that night. As terrified as I was, something inside me felt *strong*. I had never felt more frightened and out of control—but that didn't matter. Something arose in me that was much bigger than my terror.

I learned that being a man is not a formula to figure out or a secret to be uncovered. There is no missing piece to my soul that must be reapplied the way a severed limb is reattached to a body. The real problem is not that which I lack. Rather the real tragedy has been my refusal to live out that which is most true about me.

OF ADAM

I learned that a man is designed to live for someone else. But throughout my life, my feelings of inadequacy had convinced me to live for myself. I think I would have handled my son's emergency differently if it had happened only a few years earlier. I probably would have handed him over to the doctor and then hidden in some shadowy corner of the hospital until the emergency was over. For a brief moment—and without trying—I had become the man I always wanted to be. My feelings of inadequacy were no longer an excuse to shy away from being present and powerful for my son and my wife.

For the past five years, I have been able to speak hopefully. I do not speak or live perfectly; in fact, as I write this chapter I am painfully aware of my insecurities and failures. But something has changed for me. I have found hope that I would like to share with you. This hope is not a code to be followed carefully but a mysterious story to enter.

My hope springs from two truths:

I Am Inadequate

For years, I pretended I was adequate. But I was playing a game. There were, in my past, devastating circumstances that told me I was deficient. To admit such a deficiency, however, meant death for me. Even though I felt inadequate in everything, I put up a competent front. I was a little boy in a man's suit.

I hesitated to get married, have children, or develop significant friendships, because I didn't have a clue about being a man. All my inadequacies convinced me I was not up to the task. My definition of a man was one who never fears, who always feels adequate. So I worked hard to compensate for my weakness. I collected graduate degrees. I graduated at the top of my class. I strove to be one of the best teachers on campus. But all these achievements did not do the job. I still felt deficient. I believed that the day I would be a man would be the day I felt adequate—the day all my deficiencies were gone. Indeed, my most consuming obsession in life was to conquer my inadequacy. Then I could be the man I always dreamed of being.

But is this God's definition of being a man?

Remember Adam during the temptation. He lived in a perfect world. The serpent was something entirely new to him. And we have no indication that God warned Adam about the serpent. Adam probably had no clue as to how he should have responded. In short, *he was not adequate for the task*.

But Adam *could* have been present, he could have been powerful, he could have remembered what God had commanded.

When chaos intrudes into my world, I want to know the right answer. I have to know the right way to act before I will do so. *I want to be adequate.*

You may wonder: why didn't God speak up at the temptation? Indeed, there are two silent characters in Genesis 3: Adam *and* God. God does not speak in Genesis 3. He did not remove the confusion of Adam's life or the chaos of his world. The plain fact is that God showed a profound respect for Adam. *He required him to be a man.*

God does not remove my confusion, either. All my life, I desired—I *begged*—God to remove the chaos of my world so I could become a man. I wanted him to flip a switch in my soul so I could change. I would not move forward in my world until I felt adequate.

Yet my hesitancy was no small thing in God's eyes. In fact, it was actually a violation of God's intention for me. The chaos of life is God's gift to men. Without confusion and tragedy, we would never be the men God designed us to be. Through it all, he requires us to trust in him, not in ourselves. And my furious demand to be adequate was a way of trusting in myself rather than in God. For years, my feelings of inadequacy kept me from being powerful in the lives of others, because I would not trust God to help me move through the chaos of my world.

John Steinbeck tells a revealing story in his book *Cannery Row*. Two men in the novel are discussing another character named Henri the painter. Henri is a strange man, and for the most part he is a dreamer. But he does one thing well: he builds boats. Henri is a master craftsman who spends most of his life building a boat on a vacant lot. For years, he collects materials—lumber, paint, brass, screws, nails—to build a magnificent boat. And Steinbeck says this of Henri: "As a boat builder he was superb. Henri was a wonderful craftsman. The boat was sculpted rather than built."

But there is one problem. Henri never finishes his boats. He builds them beautifully and perfectly, but he refuses to finish them. Whenever he is close to completing his boat, he changes directions and starts building a new and different boat.

Here is the conversation the two characters have about Henri:

> Doc chuckled. "He still building his boat?"
>
> "Sure," said Hazel. "He's got it all changed around. New kind of a boat. I guess he'll take it apart and change it. Doc—is he nuts?"

Doc swung his heavy sack of starfish to the ground and stood panting a little. "Nuts?" he asked. "Oh, yes, I guess so. Nuts about the same amount we are, only in a different way."

Such a thing had never occurred to Hazel. He looked upon himself as a crystal pool of clarity and on his life as a troubled glass of misunderstood virtue. Doc's last statement had outraged him a little.

"But that boat—" he cried. "He's been building that boat for seven years that I know of. The blocks rotted out and he made concrete blocks. Every time he gets it nearly finished, he changes it and starts over again. I think he's nuts. Seven years on a boat."

Doc was sitting on the ground, pulling off his rubber boots. "You don't understand," he said gently. "Henri loves boats, but he's afraid of the ocean."

I have built many boats in my lifetime. And I have built some of them masterfully. As I stated earlier in my beginning story, I had achieved some of my most cherished dreams by age twenty-eight. But I built those achievements in areas that were not primary. Instead I was building in the areas that were safe to me—teaching, preaching, education. When it came to the areas that matter most—marriage, children, friends—I was terrified. Oh, I looked like I was building: I frantically sawed the boards, planed the trim, and assembled the hardware. And I probably looked like a man as I was doing it all. But I felt like a boy. I was afraid of the ocean, so I worked to convince myself that I was not. I labored hard to overcome my inadequacy as a man, because I would not sail the ocean until I believed myself to be adequate.

Like every man, I struggle with inadequacy. What are we to do with it?

My Inadequacy Is My Strength

Godly men are broken men. They have nothing to prove and nothing to lose. They take risks. They exercise great faith. They are passionate lovers.

The way of the world is to be strong in the strong places. But this is gentile leadership. Gentile leadership involves strong men lording it over weaker people. It is powerful men using others for their own benefit.

But God calls us to be strong in the broken places. When we define ourselves in terms of our brokenness rather than our strength, we follow the example of the only perfect man. He described his calling in life this way: "Behold, we are going up to Jerusalem, and the Son of Man will be handed over to the chief priests and scribes, and they will condemn him to die. They will deliver him over to the Gentiles. They will mock him, and spit upon him, and flog him, and kill him" (Matthew 20:18–19 author's translation).

The Son of Man—the perfect man—came to be delivered into the hands of his enemies, to be betrayed by those he loved. He came to set up his kingdom through his death, not through apparent strength. He deliberately gave himself over to those who—he knew—would kill him.

I, however, live in a way that ensures that I will never be betrayed. When my wife tells me I am wrong, I argue her into a corner. I am like an attorney on retainer, prepared to retaliate against any attack. I will not give my heart freely, lest someone betray me. I understand the seriousness of living in a brutal world, and that a man who gives of himself will only sacrifice himself in the end. On this side of heaven, chaos will always win.

But our calling as men is no different from that of our Master. Growing up in my world has taught me that only the strong, hardened, tough men survive and become successful. Christ—through his teaching and his life—has taught us that we are strongest in our most broken places.

I viewed my broken places—the early loss of my father, my deep-seated insecurities, my dark moods, my propensity to silence, my fear of intimacy—as excuses to live a loveless life. But when I refuse to be broken, to be betrayed, I remain the little boy in the suit. It is only my brokenness that brings me life. Being broken over my tragedies and my sin allows me to be the man I was called to be long ago in the mind of God.

Godly men are broken men. If we understood this truth, there would be no affairs, no divorces. We would not abuse our children or someone else's children. We would not be in prisons. Instead we would remind our children of the story of God. If we were willing to die for others, then maybe there would be no more starving children in Somalia or orphans in Rwanda. There would be no more violence. It would be a better world.

What story will you tell?

We will tell stories in heaven. What story will you tell? Will you sadly detail the life of a stubborn man who never allowed himself to be disabled by the tragic or sinful things in his life? Will you describe a man who was too fearful to trust God?

I hope to tell a different kind of story. My story will not be about a God who removed the chaos of my life. My story will be, in essence, that in spite of this—and in spite of all the obstacles, confusion, and fears—I trusted

God. I will say that he never took away my insecurities, but by his grace I found the courage to trust him anyway. And look what he did through me! Can you believe it? He used my weaknesses—all of them—to bring glory to himself!

What will enable each of us to tell stories like that? What will enable us to be godly men? The question really should be, *Who* makes this possible for us?

The Second Adam intruded into our world centuries ago and did what the first Adam failed to do: he stepped into the chaos and slew the serpent of old. The Second Adam, the Word incarnate, reversed the work of the first Adam.

And now I have the opportunity to live in the image of the Second Adam. I can speak. I can love. I can be present, and my presence can bring others out of their suffocating silence.

> And though this world, with devils filled
> Should threaten to undo us: We will not fear
> For God hath willed his truth to triumph through us;
> The Prince of Darkness grim, we tremble not for him,
> His rage we can endure.
> For Lo! His doom is sure, *one little word shall fell him.*
>
> —Martin Luther, "A Mighty Fortress Is Our God"

LARRY CRABB

Now at age fifty, I believe that life is far messier, and immeasurably more difficult, than I thought at twenty or thirty or even forty. (What on earth will I believe when I'm sixty or eighty? I'm counting on more faith by then.)

Let me give you a glimpse of what my life now feels like—with its darkness, with my fear, with more difficult but meaningful movement than ever before, with Christ, with following him toward manhood.

The dark nights are as black as a cave; they are less frequent and less lengthy than before but darker than ever. Before, there was always a nightlight. Now I stand in a darkness so thick I can feel it—unable to see, afraid to move, groping for the switch on the wall, or the flashlight on the desk. When I'm in that darkness, looking for a light I can turn on is the only movement I risk.

And then I find it: the familiar light switch halfway up the wall, two inches from the door. I flip it. Nothing. The power is out. I feel the desk and run my hand over it till it touches the flashlight. Dead batteries.

So I stand there, in the confusion of a world that makes no visible sense, bewildered about what I am to do next. I've lost interest in exploring the darkness. Every time I try to feel my way around the room, I scrape my knee on something sharp or bang my head on something hard. I hurt and feel dizzy. The darkness has lost its fascination. It no longer feels like the adventure of poking around in the attic of an old house. That was fun. This room feels haunted. Movement seems dangerous. I've learned to stand still.

But you can only stand still for so long. Some movement seems necessary. My mind begins to work. "I wonder how I got here. Things used to be simpler and clearer and much, much happier. Perhaps if I can figure out the path that led me to this terrible room, I can retrace my steps and get out of here."

My counseling mind kicks into gear. "Let's see, when I was six, my mother . . . In the car that day, Dad . . . The image is still clear to me of the time when . . ."

Pretty soon I feel tired. Following these kinds of thoughts feels less like retracing a path and more like wandering in a maze.

Then I hear a friend calling my name: "I'm in the room next door. There's some light in here. Maybe you can follow my voice out of your room into mine."

I feel hope. I know my friend. He is kind and clever. He can at least see where he's going and what he's doing. Maybe he can lead me to the light.

He speaks again. "From where I am, I can see that the darkness surrounding you has two sources: the room itself (How did you ever get there?) and your own heart (which, I fear, is much darker than you think). If we can understand the nature of your darkness, the understanding itself may lighten things up. Let's look first at the room. Where you are is so hopelessly confusing. You must accept that fact. There really are no clear guidelines for moving to get what you want. Facing that may help.

"And your heart. I wonder if there are forces within you that you've never admitted. Perhaps you need to take a hard look at what you're really like. You can be very demanding. And petty. Sometimes you're very arrogant. Now don't be discouraged. There's lots of good in you, too. Your life has blessed many, and I'm one of that group. Perhaps if you see both the good and the bad inside you, you'll have reason to feel excited, and you'll know what it is about you that should cause brokenness. Maybe that will illuminate the path you're to take."

The longer he talks, the less interested I become. If I told him that, I'm afraid he would call it resistance. I call it boredom. There is something to be fascinated with, but this isn't it. I'm tired of listening to the stuff that intrigues most counselors.

Then, with the resignation of an employee returning to work after a coffee break, I remind myself of my responsibilities. Even in the dark, I can find ways to sin. Maybe my body can't move, but my mind sure can. Sexual fantasies have their appeal; angry images invite themselves into my awareness.

I tell myself, "No, this isn't right. I must control these thoughts. I will replace them with prayers for others who are in darkness and for those living in artificial light."

My good resolve feels heavy, like a load I once dropped but have now picked up again. This can't be the route to joy.

Here I am, fifty years old, a Christian for more than four decades, a psychologist, teacher, and author—and I'm standing paralyzed in a dark room. It's time to take stock, in a way that I couldn't do outside this awful room. Maybe I'm in a good place to learn that which can only be learned in the dark.

Light sources that used to be dependable offer no help. Movement is impossible. Evaluating darkness—both in my soul and in the world—promises to reveal only more confusion. Moral determination is a good thing, of course, but chosen goodness seems impossible to achieve.

So what am I to do? I'm fifty, standing—like a mannequin—in a dark room, uncertain of what time will bring, wanting with all my heart to *do* something, wanting anything besides this crushing passivity.

I reflect back on the grinning rascal I pictured for you in the beginning pages of this book. And I wonder who I am now, in light of what I claim to believe.

As a kid, I had two big problems: first, I was terrified of my calling to live as a man in this uncertain world; second, I couldn't escape it. My grin hid my fear. My "rascalness" was an immature expression of the calling I couldn't escape, the calling to move the way only I could move. Both the grin and the rascalness kept the lights on. Now the lights are out. Is that good? Is the grin gone, the rascal now a mover? Am I changing into a laughing poet who lives out God's character through my uniqueness?

My wife of nearly thirty years tells me I don't laugh as well now, or as often, as I used to. I feel more serious to her. And it's not good. I sometimes approach life as a burdensome chore, an all-compelling duty that won't permit laughter. She wishes I approached it as though it were a wild adventure: full of ups and downs that, like an old-fashioned movie, move toward a final act of heroism that puts everything right. I guess the laughter part isn't going too well. And I can't find the way back to a child's mischievous grin.

The poetry part has its problems, too. A few glimpses of God's life-giving strength sneak out through the muddle of my existence. Not many, but maybe a few more now than before.

And yet, in the middle of all this, I find myself encouraged: not by any look in the mirror but by an upward glance that sees a beautiful picture, like a child seeing a graceful horse in white clouds. Only this horse is really there.

I haven't seen Christ yet, but I'm looking for him like I never have before. Sometimes I recognize his outline. More importantly, I now believe that he is there to be seen, that he wants to be seen, and that I will see him: perhaps, in this life, I won't see him fully, but maybe pretty close.

I sense his passion; I feel his movement. I think that I know a little of that which he wants to see develop in my wife and sons and a few friends. And I really think that he can use me to help make it happen, not the way a basketball coach uses his star on a crucial play but more the way Christ fed a big crowd with a little lunch.

It's hard to grin in the dark room. There's no one there to see it. The grin, I now realize, was for an audience. It feels so much less important now to impress or entertain anyone. The laughter still isn't there, but—like someone who catches on to a joke long after the punch line is delivered—I'm going to laugh. I know it's coming. It just takes me a while.

And this rascally determination to not conform is, I think, maturing into a freedom to follow my call: that unique call on *my* life that means fewer seminars, more time for thinking, reading books that stretch me rather than merely inform me, more long talks with a few people one-on-one.

During those dark nights, I still can't see a thing when I look around. The darkness is too dark. But I can hear. And sometimes I hear the unmistakable voice of God. It's not in the wind or the fire or the earthquake. The darkness has made me stand still enough to hear the gentle whisper.

And it's sweet and strong and good.

I *want* to do what it says, even though it means I must move in this terrifying darkness. I see my wife, who is no longer youthful, as more beautiful than ever. My children feel less like two reasons to worry and more like two welcome opportunities for continued investment and enjoyment.

Money is still too important, but the prospect of truly ministering to people is catching up. This world is becoming less and less comfortable. And as it does a light from heaven begins to break into the darkness. I see it. I want to follow it. I want to walk faithfully on the path it illuminates. I want to go home—as a MAN!